CREATING
CONTENT
WITH YOUR
TABLET

CREATING CONTENT
WITH YOUR
TABLET

Susan J. Brooks-Young

CORWIN
A SAGE Company

CORWIN
A SAGE Company

FOR INFORMATION

Corwin
A SAGE Company
2455 Teller Road
Thousand Oaks, California 91320
(800) 233-9936
www.corwin.com

SAGE Publications Ltd.
1 Oliver's Yard
55 City Road
London, EC1Y 1SP
United Kingdom

SAGE Publications India Pvt. Ltd.
B 1/I 1 Mohan Cooperative Industrial Area
Mathura Road, New Delhi 110 044
India

SAGE Publications Asia-Pacific Pte. Ltd.
3 Church Street
#10–04 Samsung Hub
Singapore 049483

Executive Editor: Arnis Burvikovs
Associate Editor: Desirée A. Bartlett
Editorial Assistant: Ariel Price
Production Editor: Amy Schroller
Copy Editor: Cate Huisman
Typesetter: Hurix Systems Pvt. Ltd.
Proofreader: Dennis Webb
Indexer: Naomi Linzer
Cover Designer: Michael Dubowe

Printed in the United States of America

A catalog record of this book is available from the Library of Congress.

ISBN 978-1-4522-7183-5

This book is printed on acid-free paper.

Certified Chain of Custody
SUSTAINABLE FORESTRY INITIATIVE
Promoting Sustainable Forestry
www.sfiprogram.org
SFI-01268

SFI label applies to text stock

13 14 15 16 17 10 9 8 7 6 5 4 3 2 1

Contents

Publisher's Acknowledgments

Corwin gratefully acknowledges the contributions of the following reviewers:

David Fife, Vice Principal
Tweedsmuir Public School
London, Ontario
Canada

Kendra Hanzlik, Teacher/ Instructional Coach
Prairie Heights Elementary
Cedar Rapids, IA

Michelle Strom, Language Arts Teacher, NBCT
Fort Riley Middle School
Fort Riley, KS

About the Author

Prior to embarking on a career as an author and consultant, **Susan J. Brooks-Young** spent more than 23 years as a preK–8 teacher, site administrator, and technology specialist at a county office of education. Since 1986, she has written articles, columns, and reviews for a variety of education journals. She has published a number of books about technology for education leaders that have received international attention. Susan works with educators internationally, focusing on practical technology-based strategies for personal productivity and effective technology implementation in classrooms. Mobile technologies and BYOD programs are areas of particular interest for her. She is a regular speaker at national and international conferences.

When not on the road, Susan and her husband divide their time between Vancouver, British Columbia, and their farm on Lopez Island in Washington State.

Introduction

You are probably wondering what qualifies me to write this book. I am a former classroom teacher and school administrator. I taught grades preK–8 and also served as an assistant principal, principal, and technology integration specialist (grades preK–12). Now I provide professional development and coaching focused on effective use of technology for teaching and learning to preK–12 educators around the world.

My first serious foray into mobile technology in classrooms was based on use of iPod Classics to share teacher-created podcasts and videos with preschool students and their parents. Apple's 2009 launch of the third generation iPod Touch expanded this work to incorporate touch technology in preK–12 education. Then, the original iPad was released on April 3, 2010. My first encounters with the iPad 1 were disappointing. I appreciated the larger screen, but everything I could do on the iPad was possible on the Touch. That said, I decided to keep an open mind and purchased an iPad 1 to see what possibilities might be there for classroom use.

In March 2011, the iPad 2 hit the market, and Motorola released a Wi-Fi version of the Xoom tablet, a type of Android tablet. I purchased one of each in the spirit of platform neutrality, and I am really glad I did, because I learned some very important things as a result. Both platforms had strengths and weaknesses. For example, seamless voice-to-text and Wi-Fi–based app updating were available on the Android tablet (the Xoom), while the iPad offered effortless app organization and screencasting capabilities. Fortunately, most of these features are available today on both platforms.

Perhaps the most significant thing I learned was that there were more similarities than differences between these devices. The iPad 2 and the Android tablet sport dual cameras, audio recording capabilities, and cross-platform access to basic productivity and utility apps. It was this awareness that led to my understanding that for me, the real value of tablets as tools for teaching and learning lay in my ability to use them to create content, not in their potential to deliver educational games or e-books. A secondary realization followed. Although tablets were originally conceived for one-to-one use, when they are used for content creation rather than content consumption, it's perfectly reasonable to use them in small groups or as part of a learning center rotation. This means that teachers and students can work in classrooms equipped with four to six tablets and have ample access to do meaningful work.

Since then, I have worked with educators across the United States and internationally who are using tablets with their students. I have repeatedly seen that there is great value in learning activities where small groups use tablets as one of several available resources, tapping student ingenuity through content creation. As the hardware and operating systems have matured, it has become easier to design projects that don't require one platform or the other. There are still occasions when this isn't the case—for example, until very recently the only way to capture a screencast on an Android tablet (like the Xoom) was to root the device (the equivalent of jailbreaking an iOS device, a process that allows users to download apps and other digital files not available in the iTunes store), which negates the warranty—but for the most part, it's increasingly possible to plan platform-neutral lessons.

Since I wrote the first draft of this book, Microsoft and other manufacturers have released tablets that run on Windows 8 RT or Pro, and I am working with schools that are adopting these devices. The realizations mentioned above continue to hold true—there are more similarities than differences, particularly when the tablets are viewed as vehicles for content creation rather than content consumption. Tablets running Windows 8 Pro are more robust than those running RT and can be used for any activity described in this book for iOS devices. Tablets running Windows 8 RT can be used for all activities except screencasting. An added benefit of Windows 8 is that new apps are becoming available through its app store every day, and users can go to the Desktop and use these tablets like a more traditional laptop.

Who Is This Book For?

First and foremost, it's for classroom teachers across all grade levels. It's not unusual to discover that teachers shy away from classroom use of tablets, because they don't have one-to-one access or feel ill-prepared to manage that much equipment at once. I'm not opposed to one-to-one initiatives, but many times small group activities can be more intellectually challenging for students and easier for teachers to supervise. This book describes manageable strategies teachers can employ to combine use of tablets—both iPad and Android—with assignments that can be adjusted across grade levels and content areas to address higher order thinking skills by challenging students to create products. References are also made to Windows 8 tablets, as appropriate.

The secondary target audience is site and central-office administrators. In order to be positioned to provide what teachers actually need to implement this type of instruction, administrators need to understand that many factors must be addressed, including professional development, infrastructure, and curriculum (not necessarily in that order). In reading and discussing the material put forth in this book, administrators will gain a more complete vision of what mobile learning looks like and how it can enhance teaching and learning.

How Is This Book Organized?

The topics covered in the book fall roughly into three sections. The first section consists of one chapter that discusses the importance of an intentional approach to reviewing and evaluating apps for classroom use. It includes a rationale for using a process for app review and selection, examples of existing rubrics and checklists as well as tips for app selection, and practical suggestions for collaborating with colleagues on this important work.

The second section is composed of six chapters. Five of these chapters each focus on a different strategy for creating content using mobile tablets (iPad and Android, with references to Windows 8 tablets as appropriate), including an overview of the strategy, apps that can be used to support the strategy, and practical ideas for classroom implementation. The sixth chapter in this section discusses a few additional strategies that may not be cross-platform but merit mentioning nonetheless.

The final chapter of the book provides a wrap-up of concepts presented throughout the book by presenting a model for developing lessons that rely on use of mobile apps to support content creation. In addition to a brief discussion of research on effective use of technology to support instructional activities, the model includes tables to complete during planning along with explanations for each field in the tables. The tables provided in the model are open ended to ensure applicability regardless of the hardware and apps being used.

Special Features

Discussion questions are also included at the end of every chapter. These can be used to lead group talks in faculty and staff meetings, to provide guidance in planning committees, or in a variety of adult learning situations. And, each chapter includes extensive bibliographic references for further reading. Every effort has been made to provide up-to-date web addresses (universal resource locators, or URLs) for these references. However, due to the changing face of the Internet, it is not possible to avoid listing sites that may be updated in ways that include new URLs. In this case, it is nearly always possible to find the site or article by searching using the title as the keyword(s). Finally, the last chapter includes a model for developing lesson plans that rely on use of mobile apps.

Tablet technology holds a great deal of promise for classrooms. There are other books that focus on use of iOS devices in classrooms—primarily recommending apps that students can use to automate more traditional learning activities. This book is different. Readers are encouraged to think about ways multiple tablet devices can be used to help students strengthen skills in higher order thinking and collaboration—critical areas to ensure success for today's students. It is my hope that this book will provide a springboard for educators to begin realizing the possibilities.

There's an App for That!

This morning while eating breakfast, I skimmed several news articles, read and answered a couple of e-mails, looked at a weather forecast, and checked out a book from our local library. I did not actually pick up a newspaper, boot up my laptop, watch a television program, or drop everything to run to the village. What I did do was turn on a tablet device and use four different apps that allowed me to quickly run through the tasks listed above. I didn't even open a web browser to get the jobs done!

Mobile devices are changing not just the way people communicate with one another, but also when and where they use hardware and the Internet. It wasn't too long ago that technology-supported tasks such as shopping online or using a word processor to write a report were confined to those times when it was easy to use a networked desktop or laptop computer. Rapid adoption of wireless and cell phone connectivity gave owners more flexibility. But these days, tablets (and other mobile devices as well) make it possible to engage in technology-supported activities literally anytime, anywhere.

Why does this matter to educators? Our students' use of technology outside of school continues to grow—in large part due to mobile devices—and there is increasing pressure to embrace use of these technologies, particularly tablets, in the classroom. One factor driving interest in tablets is the app. This chapter provides an overview of apps, strategies for selecting appropriate apps for use in school, and suggestions for tools educators can use when choosing apps for classroom use. As is the case whenever possible throughout this book, the discussion here is platform neutral. Ideas presented apply to iOS and Android OS devices as well as tablets that run other operating systems, including Windows 8 RT or Pro.

Apps—An Overview

The term *app* is short for *application* and refers to special software programs used on mobile devices, including tablets. Unlike traditional software programs designed to handle a variety of tasks, apps are created to carry out specific, discrete functions. Some apps require an Internet connection, while others will work with or without the Internet. Tablets generally come with a few preinstalled apps, such as calendars, maps, games, calculators, and address books. But these are just the beginning.

Hundreds of thousands of apps created by third-party developers are available for use on a variety of tablets. Unlike computer software, which can be purchased on CD-ROM discs, apps can only be downloaded from online stores. For example, owners of iPads use a computer or the tablet itself to access the virtual iTunes App Store, where they purchase apps using an Apple ID. Owners of Android tablets also use a computer or mobile device to access online app stores, including Google Play and the Amazon App Store. Microsoft hosts an app store for owners of its mobile devices as well.

Most apps cost little or nothing, with prices typically ranging from $0.99 to $10. There are a few apps with much higher price tags, but these tend to be very specialized in nature. For instance, Proloquo2Go, an app that turns an iPad into a full-featured communication device for users with speaking difficulties, runs $189.99. Although most educators probably won't need to spend nearly $200 on an app, it is important to keep in mind that the ongoing cost of even inexpensive apps mounts up quickly. As a result, any plan to implement use of tablets on campus needs to include policies for purchasing apps.

Apple offers an App Store Volume Purchase program for educational institutions. Just recently, Google announced Google Play for Education. According to the company's press release, this is "an extension of the Google Play Store for schools, adding curation, bulk purchasing, and instant distribution to students' Android tablets for educational apps, books and videos" (Sadauskas, 2013). And, Microsoft in Education offers Academic Volume Licensing.

HOW WILL APPS BE USED?

Before purchasing apps, it is important to reach an agreement about how apps will be used to support instruction and the kinds of apps that best support that use. Will students be using apps to practice and review skills? Will they play education games and simulations or use productivity apps to complete work? What about as a substitute for textbooks? The underlying premise of this book is that, in terms of potential for academic growth, the most effective use of tablets is for content creation rather than content consumption. Apps that support content creation are those that allow users to make a product, not just play a game or practice rote skills. Apps of this type may be preinstalled on tablets—*Camera* is an example of one such app, or downloaded from an app store—for example, *iTalk, Voice Recorder,* or *Audio Recorder.*

This doesn't mean that it's never appropriate to use a tablet to practice skills or automate tasks that have previously been accomplished in another way. However, when content consumption is the primary reason tablets are brought into classrooms, the technology is probably not being used to its greatest advantage. This is because this type of tablet use nearly always falls into the lowest levels of the Revised Bloom's Taxonomy. Chapter 8 includes a discussion of models and research that support student use of technology to engage in learning based on use of higher order thinking skills as well as a form that can be used to guide educators in designing activities that incorporate thoughtful use of apps into instruction.

FINDING THE RIGHT APP

It's easy to succumb to the glitz of the app world. A slick interface can be more attractive to a user than the actual benefits derived from using an app. Educators must be particularly aware of this pitfall. There are thousands of apps that are interesting, engaging, fun, and inexpensive and yet have no place in the classroom. In many respects, early ventures into classroom use of tablets are reminiscent of the early days of classroom use of desktop computers, when, due to a lack of high-quality instructional resources, available software often drove instruction, although curricular needs should have been informing software selection.

How to begin looking for apps that would work well in the classroom? Online app stores are difficult to navigate if you don't already have an app name or don't have a good idea of the specific type of app you're looking for. One way to find apps is to conduct an Internet search using keywords that identify the content area, grade level, and tablet operating system for apps that might be of interest. There are also many curated lists of apps available online. For example, the *iPod Touch* and *iPad Resources LiveBinder, Android Resources LiveBinder,* and the *Windows 8 Tablet Resources LiveBinder* cited in Additional Resources at the end of this chapter offer app lists from a wide variety of resources. Once specific app titles are located, it's easy to implement a process for reviewing apps for classroom use.

There are thousands of "educational" apps on the market, and the quality of these apps varies widely. Why is this so? Anyone can develop an app and submit it to an app store to be considered for inclusion in that store's list of available apps. Yes, apps do go through a vetting process, but they are primarily evaluated on whether or not they function the way the app developer claims they will. Being selected for the store doesn't mean the content of the app is any good—just that the app works. (And some purchasers might even argue that point!) The credentials of the app developer are not evaluated.

Given this background information, how do educators identify top notch apps? There are two strategies that are very helpful. The first relates to ways to initially identify apps to explore more fully, and the second relates to use of a rubric or checklist to evaluate apps prior to use with students. The first strategy is probably adequate on its own when looking for apps to use for personal productivity. Both steps are necessary before using an app for instructional purposes.

Strategy 1: Price is not necessarily an indication of quality, so it's important to do your homework prior to purchasing apps. Refunds are difficult, if not impossible, to come by. This is not an issue when the app is free, but when you're purchasing to test, it does make a difference. Therefore, it behooves you to do as much preliminary checking as possible.

There are several ways to vet new apps before buying. Online app stores invite customers to rate their purchases, and this information can be helpful to potential customers. App reviews frequently appear on a variety of websites. A quick Internet search using the title of each app of interest as well as the keywords "app review" and the name of the operating system you're interested in (e.g., iOS, Android, Windows 8) will almost always result in one or more reviews. Finally, some apps are available in "lite" versions that allow potential customers to try out an app before buying the full version. In addition, the Amazon App Store has a feature that allows customers to try out an app online before making a purchase, and developers of Windows 8 apps are allowed to include a "try before you buy" option.

Once you've downloaded a new app, put it through its paces. If it's an app for personal productivity, try out the various features to see if it will work for you. Use the app in a work-related activity as soon as possible. It's probably best to tackle new productivity apps one at a time to give yourself a chance to really integrate each one's use into your work life and to avoid becoming overwhelmed. If it's an app for instructional use, definitely take the time to work through Strategy 2.

Strategy 2: Apps you plan to use for instruction warrant a far more systemic approach to evaluation prior to use in class. For example, free apps often include ads and in-app purchases—neither is appropriate for student use. In addition, just as with any other apps you download, it is important to test all the features of the app. If there are ways to make correct or incorrect responses, test both to see what happens in each situation. This is more important than you may think. Why? One reason for using some apps is to give students more autonomy as they work through an activity. However, if the feedback they receive while using the app is vague or incomplete, it will lead to confusion and frustration.

Also, there are times when the negative response is more attractive than the response for a correct answer. For example, there is a preschool app where a cartoon character does a happy dance when students get an answer correct. But when the answer they select is incorrect, the character gives them the raspberry and spits. Which response do you suppose most self-respecting preschoolers will want to see repeatedly? That's right; they will choose incorrect answers over and over in order to see the response for wrong answers!

Work through multiple levels to make sure the progression of stages of difficulty is instructionally sound. Look for ways to monitor student activity while using the app. Most important, throughout your review, ask yourself how this app supports the curriculum. You need to have a checklist or rubric to use while evaluating apps for student use. Several examples are readily available online that can be used as-is or revised to meet local criteria or need. Rubrics go into greater depth, but checklists are easier to complete.

Depending on the ages of your students or the content area you teach, it might be better to work with colleagues in an academic department or in a grade level group. Be proactive! Regardless of the makeup of your work group, it's better to devise your own review process than to have one thrust upon you in the wake of some kind of app selection mishap. If an app selection process is already in place at your school or within your district, make sure it focuses on what's really important—how the app ties to the curriculum and how it can be used to support teaching and learning. If revisions are needed, do what you can to become part of the solution.

App rubrics and checklists often name a specific device in the title, but most are actually platform agnostic. If you are looking for samples to review, here is a list of several that can be used as-is or easily modified to meet local needs. Links are provided in the References and Additional Resources section of this chapter.

- *Evaluation Rubric for iPod/iPad Apps:* Originally developed by Harry Walker (Johns Hopkins University), this rubric was edited by Kathy Schrock and measures seven domains on a scale of 1–4 points.
- *iPad App Assessment Rubric for Librarians:* This Google Form identifies three categories for app evaluation—Support for Learning, App Usability, and App Quality. Directions for adding a copy of the form to your Google Drive are provided.
- *TCEA App Evaluation Rubric:* Similar to the Evaluation Rubric for iPod/iPad Apps, this rubric includes six domains and uses a 1–4 point scale.
- *Ways to Evaluate Educational Apps:* This blog post by Tony Vincent includes links to several rubrics and checklists educators can use to review apps.

Notice that the first item in each of these samples asks about the tie to the curriculum—asking how the app relates to the content you are supposed to be teaching. Whether you decide to use an existing rubric or checklist or to design your own, this should always be the first question. No matter how engaging the app is, if the relationship with the curriculum isn't crystal clear, do not use the app with your students.

Speaking of whom, it's also a good idea to ask a couple of students to test apps for you. Not only will they find ways to push apps to their limits, they will also be able to give you an honest assessment from their perspective of apps' staying power in terms of student engagement. The additional reviews take time but are critical to effective classroom use of mobile devices.

APP AND FILE MANAGEMENT

App selection is just the beginning. Once apps are identified, someone must take responsibility for purchasing, downloading, distributing, and organizing them. Sam Gliksman, a consultant who assists schools in planning iPad implementations, has published an extensive list of items schools need to consider when making decisions about a deployment. Rather than repeat his article here, I have included his list in the Additional Resources at the end of this chapter for readers to reference. Be sure to review the following sections: Group Device Management, Individual Device Management, Application Purchase and Management, and Content Management. Not every point pertains to this discussion, but in each section at least one does. Although Gliksman references iPads, many of his suggestions are relevant no matter what type of tablet is being considered.

In my experience, failure to establish this type of procedure prior to launching a tablet initiative nearly always leads to limited or stalled implementation. App management is a time-consuming task. The person designated to manage apps must have the time and technical skills to do the job as well as access to an infrastructure robust enough to get the work done as efficiently as possible. It is also important that teachers have ready access to the app manager to address problems and questions as they arise.

At schools where tablets are used to create content, teachers and tech staff also need to sort out how files created on the tablet will be managed. There are a variety of apps that can be used for students to share files with their teachers and peers, such as *Box, Dropbox,* and *Edmodo,* but these need to be discussed and adopted before students begin creating content on the tablets. Not only will accounts need to be established for whatever options are selected, but an e-mail address will need to be associated with each device to enable it to send files elsewhere. All of this is manageable, but it needs to be resolved prior to implementation on the initiative.

Discussion Points

1. What kinds of apps do you use on your personal tablet? Which of those apps are most useful to you and why?

2. What apps are currently downloaded on student devices? How were these apps selected?

3. What is your site or district policy related to purchasing, downloading, and updating apps? How well does this policy work on a day-to-day basis? Explain your answer.

4. Select one or more of the app selection rubrics or checklists referenced in this chapter. Modify the tool for use at your site, and then test it by reviewing two or three apps. Compare your ideas and results with colleagues.

REFERENCES AND ADDITIONAL RESOURCES

Apps and reports/articles mentioned in this chapter are listed here, as are additional resources that offer further information about topics discussed in this chapter.

Apps

Apple in Education. http://bit.ly/o6dRNq
Microsoft in Education. http://www.microsoft.com/education/ww/buy/Pages/index.aspx
Box. https://www.box.com/
Dropbox. https://www.dropbox.com/
Edmodo. http://www.edmodo.com/mobile/

Websites

Android Resources LiveBinder. http://goo.gl/O6I8P
iPod Touch & iPad Resources LiveBinder. http://goo.gl/OmpTc
Microsoft Academic Volume Licensing. http://goo.gl/EQOcd
Windows 8 Tablet Resources LiveBinder. http://goo.gl/HJ829

Rubrics and Checklists

Evaluation Rubric for iPod/iPad Apps. http://kathyschrock.net/pdf/ipad_app_rubric.pdf
iPad App Assessment Rubric for Librarians. http://www.livebinders.com/play/play?id=36989backurl=/shelf/my
TCEA App Evaluation Rubric. http://www.tcea.org/documents/PD/TCEA%20App%20Evaluation%20Rubric.pdf
Vincent, T. (n.d.). *Ways to evaluate educational apps.* Retrieved from http://learninginhand.com/blog/ways-to-evaluate-educational-apps.html

Online Reports and Articles

Beware the app. (2010, November 30). *Education Apps Review.* Retrieved from http://www.iear.org/iear/tag/rubric
Gliksman, S. (2011, February 24). *Preparing your school for an iPad implementation.* iPads in Education. Retrieved from http://ipadeducators.ning.com/profiles/blogs/preparing-your-school-for-an
Roscorla, T. (2012, May 14). *12 keys to finding quality education apps.* Center for Digital Education. Retrieved from http://www.centerdigitaled.com/classtech/12-Keys-Education-Apps.html
Sadauskas, A. (2013, June 25). *Google Play for Education now open for app developers.* Smartcompany. Retrieved from http://www.smartcompany.com.au/information-technology/056180-google-play-for-education-now-open-for-app-developers.html

Photography
and Tablets

A class of middle school students is reading *Flowers for Algernon*. Instead of writing a summary of each chapter, they are working in small groups to stage and shoot five photographs that depict the main ideas or events in each chapter. They may not use text to get their points across, just images.

Elementary-aged English language learners need to learn very specific vocabulary words for a science lesson. Working in trios, they use tablet devices and an app called *Skitch* to take photos of objects related to the lesson and then add the correct vocabulary term to each photo. They share their collections for studying.

High school geometry students are not engaged in a lesson on diameter and circumference. Their teacher decides to regroup. She asks students to work in pairs for the next 24 hours to take photos of circles in everyday life and post them on the cloud. The next day, diameter and circumference are revisited using the images students posted. This time the discussion is lively, as students realize why they might care about the circumference of the tires on their cars or how many 16-inch pizzas they need to order for a party.

Use of photography in the classroom is common practice. For decades, teachers have employed photos for a variety of instructional purposes, particularly since the advent of inexpensive digital cameras. In her book, *Teaching and Learning with Digital Photography: Tips and Tools for Early Childhood Classrooms*, Linda Good points out that many well-known developmental theories of experts like Maslow, Piaget, and Montessori support use of images in teaching and learning a variety of skills, beginning with very young children (2009). Initially—more often than not—the images found in classrooms were the work of adults, but inexpensive point-and-click digital cameras make it practical for even our youngest students to create images of their own.

This capability results in greater levels of intricacy in classroom activities that rely on the use of photography. And now that most tablet devices sport at least one camera, teachers and students often have access to multiple digital cameras at one time, significantly increasing the ease of implementation of this kind of activity. The focus of this chapter is on still photography. Chapter 3 concentrates on creating video. But before exploring strategies for having students work with images, let's take a quick look at the concept of visual literacy and its impact on student learning.

VISUAL LITERACY

According to Wikipedia (2012), *visual literacy* can be defined as

the ability to interpret, negotiate, and make meaning from information presented in the form of an image, extending the meaning of literacy, which commonly signifies interpretation of a written or printed text. Visual literacy is based on the idea that pictures can be 'read' and that meaning can be communicated through a process of reading.

I would venture to say that in today's visual world, it's equally important for students to understand how images are created and to fully understand that images can be—and often are—manipulated or altered to elicit specific responses from viewers. Visual literacy encompasses more than photography, but for purposes of this chapter, this is where we will focus.

Image manipulation has existed since the early days of photography—there are many documented examples. Some manipulations are not malicious. For example, the October 2012 photographs of sharks swimming through New Jersey neighborhoods in the wake of Hurricane Sandy fooled many, but weren't meant to cause damage to anyone (Mikkelson & Mikkelson, 2012). But in other instances, the intent is to deceive viewers and harm individuals or institutions. One famous example of malevolent manipulation of an image comes from the 2004 US presidential election. In this case, a photo was published purportedly depicting Senator John Kerry and actor Jane Fonda sharing the stage during an anti–Vietnam War rally. The photo appeared to be genuine, but it was actually created by combining two photographs, one taken in New York in 1971, and the other in Florida in 1972. The sole purpose of the doctored photograph was to cause harm to then-presidential candidate, John Kerry (Mikkelson & Mikkelson, 2004).

Common sense and a little detective work are often enough to determine the legitimacy of an image, but not always. In a world where digital photography is ubiquitous, businesses such as Fourandsix are springing up, offering image authentication services to law enforcement agencies and other clients. An effective strategy for helping students learn to be critical viewers of images is to incorporate use of photography into a variety of learning activities. But where to begin?

Depending on the age of your students and your purpose in using photography in learning activities, you may want to spend time teaching visual literacy skills prior to handing cameras to students. If you opt to go this route, a book such as *Focus on Photography: A Curriculum Guide* (Way, 2006) might be a good place to start. Although it may provide more depth than many teachers will need, the online curriculum guide is free, and it covers topics starting with visual literacy and then moving on photography basics and strategies for tying photography to the curriculum. Should you decide to plunge right into photography itself, this curriculum guide is still a valuable resource. Either way, your students will benefit from a bit of background knowledge.

CAMERA BASICS

The cameras that come on tablet devices are not suitable for professional photography. However, that does not mean that students and teachers cannot get a great deal of use out of the cameras. Many tablets sport dual cameras that can take still photos or record video. Typically, the back camera is used for shooting still photographs and video while the front camera is used for video calls using apps like *FaceTime* on an iPad or *Skype* on an iPad or Android device.

Before getting into a discussion of apps and activities, it's worth taking a little time to cover simple basics of still photography that teachers will probably need to cover with students. The intent is not to make professional photographers out of your students but to offer a few tips that will help them create better photographs than might otherwise be the case.

Here are six tips to share with students. Depending on grade level and activity, you may want to limit instruction to specific tips that will help students complete the task at hand. Not included here, but worth mentioning, are things like taking care if walking with the tablet, holding the tablet steady when shooting (the photo is taken when the shutter button is *released*, not when it's *pressed*), and pointing out that tablets do not have built-in flash capability.

1.   Composition: No matter what the quality of the camera, the photographer is the one who decides the content of the photograph. Take a few seconds to think about how the photograph

will look. In most cases, to avoid a picture that looks crooked, horizontal lines should be aligned with the horizon, and vertical lines should be perpendicular to it. Background objects—a street sign or passerby—should not interfere with the image. Finally, it's not necessary to center the subject of the photo. The rule of thirds says to use imaginary lines, two vertical and two horizontal, to divide the shot into nine equal pieces. Then place the subjects on the lines or where the lines intersect. Apps often provide an actual grid.

2. Lighting: Simple basics include not pointing the camera at a window when shooting indoors, having the sun behind you when shooting outdoors, and using the flash outdoors to fill shadows.

3. Color: Use of color impacts the way a viewer responds to a photograph. Images with contrasting colors are usually more dramatic than images with shades of the same color, which tend to be more harmonizing.

4. Point of view: It's interesting to shoot photos from varying perspectives. For example, how might a building look to an ant on the sidewalk, or what does a flower blossom look like to a bee that's just landed on a petal? Don't be afraid to try looking at something from a fresh point of view.

5. Orientation: Don't be afraid to turn the camera from a horizontal to vertical view. Some subjects look better in vertical, so turn the camera sideways, and take a look before shooting.

6. Take lots of pictures: If you're photographing people, they often look better in the second or third shot because they tend to relax after the first picture. Even if you're shooting objects or animals, you may get a better shot after the first one. Digital images are easy enough to delete, so go for it!

Despite the last tip presented here, using tablets for photography will eat up storage at an amazing rate. You need to have a plan for transferring photos from the tablets to a laptop, desktop, or other type of storage. The cloud may seem like a simple solution, and it may be initially, but if you have to pay for storage or if photos are posted publicly online, there may be issues.

I prefer connecting a tablet to a laptop, identifying the tablet as an external storage device, and then copying the photos from it. Once the photos are transferred, they can be deleted from the tablet to free up storage space there. Also, while there are many apps that support photo editing, I find it easier to edit on a computer than on a tablet; however, this is definitely a matter of personal preference.

CAMERA APPS

Tablets that have built-in cameras come with a preinstalled *Camera* app. The features of these apps are fairly simple, but they include surprises like the ability to do some simple editing. To review the features of the preinstalled *Camera* app on an iPad, download the free iPad *User Guide* from the iBooks store. To learn more about the Camera app on a tablet running Android OS 4.1, visit Get Help With Android and click on the name of your tablet type or model. Click Apps in the list of help topics that appears, and then click on Camera & Gallery. For older tablets (iPad or Android) running an earlier OS, you will need to search the Internet to find the correct user guide. Since there are several manufacturers of tablets running Windows 8, you may need to check with a specific company to get detailed camera operation information. However, a basic description for using Surface cameras is available at the Microsoft Surface Camera website.

In addition to the *Camera* app, tablets running iOS, Android, and Windows 8 come with a preinstalled photo gallery (called simply "Photos" on the iPad and Windows 8 tablet and "Gallery" on the Android). This is where you access photos stored on the tablet and also where it is possible to do some very basic photo editing. As is the case with the *Camera* app, the free user guides for iOS and Android described above explain how to navigate and use the photo gallery. These user guides also explain how to connect your tablet to a computer and transfer images. To learn more about photos on Windows 8 tablets, read *How to View Photos on Your Windows 8 Tablet* by Andy Rathbone (2013).

The iPad also boasts the preinstalled *Photo Booth* app, which enables users to apply effects as they shoot still photos within the app. Android and Windows 8 tablets do not offer a preinstalled photo effects app, but several free apps are available in the Google Play and Windows stores. One example for Android is *Photo Effects* by Dexati. Students need to be taught not to download additional apps when prompted, but there are more effects options in this app than in *Photo Booth*, and all are free. An example for Windows 8 is *Fotor* by Chengdu Everimaging Science and Technology.

The apps mentioned above are all that's needed to get started. Teachers working with older students may want to explore additional camera and photo editing apps as students' photography skills increase, but it's not required. Many free apps aren't as promising as they may appear to be initially, because the really nice features turn out to be in-app purchases. This means that the basic app is free, but the effects and capabilities that make it stand apart from the preinstalled apps are available only for a fee. On the other hand, teachers may find enough features within free apps to make them worth downloading or even have a budget to cover downloading paid apps or in-app purchases.

Here are two examples that are free, run on both Android and iOS tablets, and do not require in-app purchases to function.

- *Snapseed:* This free app runs on Android and iOS tablets. This app makes is easy for users to edit photographs on the tablet
- *PicCollage:* This is a free Android and iOS app students can use to make photo collages. Great for sharing five-photo stories and photo essays.

And here is a free app that runs on all three platforms.

- *Skitch:* Use this free app (Android, iOS, and Windows 8) to annotate, create, edit, share, and present photos.

STRATEGIES FOR CLASSROOM USE

There are a number of ways cameras can be incorporated into daily classroom use. Some are very practical strategies for documenting work or capturing notes, while other approaches encourage students to think creatively. Before launching into a brief discussion of these activities, it's important to take a moment to acknowledge that cameras can be used inappropriately, causing problems that must be nipped in the bud.

One of the realities of using any mobile technology with students is that kids will behave like kids. If they didn't, we'd all be looking for new jobs, but that doesn't make the situation easier to deal with when it arises. I've worked in a couple of schools where, prior to my involvement with their project, tablet devices equipped with dual cameras were distributed to students with no discussion about appropriate behaviors or consequences of misbehavior. The rationale given later was that the adults wanted to "see what would happen."

It probably comes as no surprise that in both cases, when left to their own devices, the middle school–aged students made poor decisions about how to use the cameras. Unfortunately, instead of seizing on this teachable moment, school leaders instructed the technology staff to disable the cameras on every tablet. Nothing further was said to students, and a prime opportunity to help them become more responsible technology users was lost.

Rather than hoping students will figure out and meet expectations about the "right" way to use the technology provided, teachers and other adults who work with students need to be prepared to spend some time setting expectations and explaining what needs to be done to meet these expectations, as well as providing clear consequences for both positive and negative student behaviors, and then monitoring students' use of the cameras. This approach requires more work up front, but it does pay off in the long run.

It may be that initially teachers will want students to use cameras for more practical tasks, such as capturing notes on a chart or whiteboard to add to a shared *Evernote* notebook, scanning and saving papers, or documenting completed student work. This approach gets students using cameras in a more directed environment, while ground rules are being established. These tasks run the gamut from documenting completed projects, to capturing notes written on charts or whiteboards, to scanning and saving documents. Once students are accustomed to using the cameras for activities that are more directed, and once they see that teachers are involved and aware of how the cameras are being used, it's easy to begin incorporating more creative uses of the cameras.

Keeping in mind that it's still important to monitor students' use of the cameras, encourage them to work together in small groups or pairs to complete assignments that rely on creativity and critical thinking. Even in classrooms where students have one-to-one access to tablets with cameras, it has been my experience that students get more out of an assignment when working with one to three other students. Preparation for this type of activity is like any collaborative learning assignment.

The premise of collaborative learning is that groups of students work together to explore a substantial question or solve a real problem. In cooperative learning, which is one type of collaborative learning, student teams work to complete a structured assignment in which they are individually and collectively responsible for completing the task (Workshop, 2004). Of the different models for cooperative learning, one that works particularly well for tablet photography is called group investigation.

Once the problem or question is identified, the class brainstorms ideas for completing the task, and then each group chooses one topic or approach. At that point, individual groups identify roles and tasks for each member to assume responsibility for. When the initial work is completed, the team creates a class presentation that is shared with—and evaluated by—the entire class (Models That Promote, 2004).

Successful cooperative learning activities require careful preplanning. It also takes time to lead students through the process, and almost inevitably there will be issues with individual and group responsibilities initially. However, the skills employed to successfully negotiate these assignments are the same skills students will need throughout their lifetimes, both personally and professionally.

ACTIVITY SUGGESTIONS

Once expectations are clear, teachers and students can use tablet photography across grade levels and content areas to present information or demonstrate learning. Younger students will require more guidance initially, and teachers may want to use class projects until students are more proficient working in small groups, but even very young children are capable of using tablet cameras in creative ways. As you plan lessons, remember to base them on meaningful learning. Do not use still photography in an attempt to engage students in activities that are marginally worthwhile, whether or not technology support is built in. Here are some ideas.

Five-photo stories: The Flickr group that originated this idea was launched in 2004. The link is provided in the References and Additional Resources section of this chapter ("Tell a Story"). This activity is completed in two parts. First, students tell a story with photos—the only text in the story is its title. Second, an audience (e.g., the class) is invited to constructively react to the story via comments or other feedback. The original Flickr group is not education specific, so there may be stories there that would not be appropriate for use with students. Visit the site ahead of time and capture some sample stories to share with the class. Then have them work in groups of two to four to create their own five-photo stories on a topic related to class studies. Post the stories on a class site where feedback can be offered.

Teachers of very young children may opt to make this a class project or to provide the story photos and ask children to react to the story. Once these children develop an understanding of the genre, they can take their own photos. This activity can be repeated multiple times using different topics.

Vocabulary development: I'm not a big fan of flashcards. However, there are many occasions when students need to master academic language related to content or basic vocabulary when learning a new language. In these instances, student-created flashcards that include images are more meaningful to students than commercially prepared study aids. There are apps for iOS and Android tablets that can be used to create flashcard collections, but quality and ease of use can be questionable.

A simple alternative is to take photographs that illustrate the vocabulary word(s) using a tablet, and then transfer the photos to a computer with slide presentation software. Paste each photo on a slide, type the word (be sure to check spelling), and add other appropriate text, such as the definition or a sentence using the word. Some slide presentation software supports audio, making it possible to also record the student's voice saying the word and giving the definition or reading a sentence. It's also possible to use slide transitions to make it appear that the vocabulary "card" has a front and back, or to use animations to make various elements of the slide appear in different order—photograph first, then label, or vice versa. Depending on the software used, it may also be possible to post the finished slides online, so they can be accessed from any Internet-connected computer. In this case, make sure audio and animations are supported. It may also be possible to use a web-based slide tool to make and post the cards.

This activity works well with students of all ages and capabilities, although younger students will need more help and monitoring initially. Over time you and your students can build flashcard collections that are available to all, regardless of who originally created them.

Concept visualization: What better way to gain perspective on how your students are thinking about a concept than to ask them to demonstrate their understanding visually using photographs? The assignment can be something as simple as taking photos to illustrate examples of various shapes in the real world after a geometry lesson or as complicated as a photo essay from the point of view of someone or something other than themselves.

Depending on students' abilities, teachers may want to begin by modeling this strategy. In this case, they would use photos they take to illustrate a concept being presented in class and then talk with students about how and why images impact learning. Once students understand how photos can be used, they work in cooperative groups to plan and create their own photographs.

This strategy works with students of all ages and in every content area. It is especially helpful for students who are strong visual or spatial learners.

Writing prompts: Have you read *The Mysteries of Harris Burdick* (Van Allsburg, 1984)? This book consists of 14 pictures, each with a title and one line of text. According to a fictional editor's note, illustrator Harris Burdick brought the pictures to a children's book editor. He promised to return the following day with the accompanying short stories, but was never seen again. Readers are encouraged to write their own short stories using the pictures as inspiration.

Challenge your students to shoot interesting photos, give each a title and one-line caption, and then trade them amongst themselves or with another class to create their own stories. Publish the short stories on a class website for feedback. It's easy to see the connection between this activity and language arts classes, but students can also take photos that serve as prompts for nonfiction writing for social studies, science, and mathematics classes as well as for classes in other disciplines.

This chapter covers just a few of the ways that tablet cameras can be used in the classroom to create content. To learn more, review the entries in the resources section below. You may also find it helpful to review and talk about the discussion points provided here.

Discussion Points

1. How has access to digital photography tools impacted you personally? Which uses are most important to you and why?

2. Brainstorm a list of ways students in your school or district could use digital photography as a tool for learning.

3. Review your site or district policy related to student use of digital cameras. Decide whether or not the existing policy is suitable for a 21st century learning environment. Explain your answer.

4. Download and experiment with at least one of the photo apps mentioned in this chapter. Describe ways you could use this app for and with students.

References and Additional Resources

Apps and reports/articles mentioned in this chapter are listed here, as are additional resources that offer further information about topics discussed in this chapter.

Apps

Android Apps. http://www.dexati.com/android.html
iTunes Preview: iBooks. http://bit.ly/TV5VDd
PicCollage. http://pic-collage.com/
Skitch. http://evernote.com/skitch/
Snapseed. http://www.snapseed.com/

Books

Good, L. (2009) *Teaching and learning with digital photography: Tips and tools for early childhood classrooms.* Thousand Oaks, CA: Corwin. Retrieved from http://bit.ly/UeBYML

Van Allsburg, C. (1984). *The mysteries of Harris Burdick.* Boston, MA: Houghton Mifflin.

Way, C. (2006). *Focus on photography: A curriculum guide.* International Center of Photography. Retrieved from http://www.icp.org/museum/education/teacher-resources

Websites

Android OS Help. http://bit.ly/TV5Dfm
Fourandsix. http://www.fourandsix.com
Surface Cameras. http://goo.gl/9txrF
Tell a Story in 5 Frames. http://www.flickr.com/groups/visualstory/

Online Reports and Articles

Digital citizenship poster for middle and high school classrooms. (2012). Digital Literacy and Citizenship Curriculum, Common Sense Media. Retrieved from http://bit.ly/WoGoQN

Mikkelson, B., & Mikkelson, D. P. (2004, March 1). *John Kerry.* Retrieved from http://www.snopes.com/photos/politics/kerry2.asp

Mikkelson, B., & Mikkelson, D. P. (2012, November 26). *Hurricane Sandy photographs.* Retrieved from http://www.snopes.com/photos/natural/sandy.asp

Models that promote cooperative learning. (1994, Fall). *Classroom compass* (p. 3). Southwest Consortium for the Improvement of Mathematics and Science Teaching. Retrieved from http://www.sedl.org/pubs/classroom-compass/cc_v1n2.pdf

Photo tampering throughout history. (n.d.). Fourandsix. Retrieved from http://www.fourandsix.com/photo-tampering-history/

Rathbone, A. (2013). How to view photos on your Windows 8 tablet. *Windows for tablets for dummies.* Retrieved from http://goo.gl/HLUZq

Workshop: cooperative and collaborative learning. (2004). Concept to Classroom, Thirteen l ed online. Retrieved from http://www.thirteen.org/edonline/concept2class/coopcollab/index.html

Using images in teaching: A quick guide. (2010, December 7). *Global Grid for Learning.* Retrieved from http://www.globalgridforlearning.com/using-images-in-teaching-a-quick-guide

Visual literacy. (2012, November 6). In *Wikipedia.* Retrieved from http://en.wikipedia.org/wiki/Visual_literacy

3

Video and Tablets

The first instructional film to find its way into US class-rooms appeared in the early 1900s. By 1913, Thomas Edison was predicting the demise of the traditional textbook in the belief that motion pictures would replace print materials as the primary source of classroom content. He was wrong; however, Edison did recognize the power of visual learning and was correct in his viewpoint that there was growing interest in this medium throughout the early part of the 20th century.

When did educational film earn serious recognition as a tool for teaching and learning? You may think that it was the filmstrips, films, and television programs used in classrooms in the 1950s that gave visual learning a real boost, but in reality, it was World War II. The United States needed to train thousands of military recruits in a very short period of time, and one of the primary instructional strategies used was viewing films and filmstrips specifically designed to teach skills in soldiering. This positive outcome created interest in use of instructional film and filmstrips in more traditional classrooms (Marshall, 2002).

Fast-forward to the 21st century. While there have been a number of bumps along the road, visual learning based on use of motion pictures is commonplace. Teachers and students rely heavily on classroom use of instructional video clips obtained from on- and offline sources. As reported by Cradler, Freeman, and Cradler (2005), a survey conducted in 2005 showed that 94% of teachers had used instructional video effectively during the school year and that most teachers were using it at least once every week. Full-length educational programs are available for viewing in the classroom or through use of Internet-connected devices. And, thanks to advances in various technologies, educators and students have ready access to affordable devices that make it feasible for them to not just view video, but create their own as well.

Early in the second chapter of this book there is a short discussion of visual literacy that also applies to this chapter. As an introduction to use of student- and teacher-created video, this chapter includes a brief discussion of viewing and creating video and why both approaches to instruction are useful.

Consuming and Creating Video

For generations of public school students in the United States, "movie day" was something very special. Teachers often designated Fridays as the time for watching filmstrips or movies related to content being covered in class. Students typically viewed whatever was on offer from beginning to end in darkened, quiet classrooms, and then they might participate in a discussion or writing activity related to whatever they'd watched.

As instructional media matured and VCRs with television sets became commonplace in classrooms, teachers increasingly encouraged students to become active viewers of whatever they were watching. This approach was supported in two ways. First, teachers could cue a video to a specific starting point or stop it whenever they liked so that they didn't need to have students watch an entire program when just a portion of it was relevant. Second, the pause feature enabled teachers to pace the video, checking for understanding and encouraging discussion throughout the program instead of waiting until the end. DVD players made this viewing method even easier, and web-based video enables teachers not only to show existing video clips but also to edit them so that they are targeted to very specific information.

And so, innovations in motion picture technology over the last 50 years have made active viewing of instructional video virtually seamless—a factor that is important to today's educators, because studies do show that watching educational programming can positively impact student performance (Cruse, 2009). This is especially true when students are engaged in active rather than passive viewing (Marshall, 2002). But even under the best of circumstances, when students are part of an audience, they are consuming content someone else made.

As mentioned in Chapter 1, the Revised Bloom's Taxonomy places "creating" at the pinnacle of the pyramid often used to depict levels of critical thinking skills related to learning (Overbaugh & Schultz, n.d.). Students who are consuming video content developed by someone else can reach "evaluating," the next-to-highest level of the taxonomy when activities are properly designed, but when students make their own video, they move to the highest level.

The benefits of creating video are many. In the course of planning and shooting video, students use real-life skills such as goal setting, project management, and working collaboratively. They practice language arts skills embedded throughout this type of project, including reading, writing, listening, and speaking, as well as skills and knowledge related to other content areas such as math, science, or social studies (depending on the assignment).

Despite the positive outcomes of students creating videos of their own, teachers sometimes shy away from this kind of activity out of concern for the amount of time it might take or due to their own lack of video production skills. Before digital cameras that could record video became available on most cell phones and tablets, these were real fears; however, these cameras are much easier to use than camcorders of the past, and making a short video doesn't necessarily need to result in an Oscar nomination–worthy product. It is entirely possible to keep the process simple, using a few basic techniques that will enable students to create their own content without it becoming a major production.

Video Basics

In the spirit of keeping video projects simple, consider limiting the length of the video to somewhere between three and five minutes. As students become more proficient at video production, this time limit can be extended. Initially, three to five minutes will seem like ample time.

The steps for making a simple video are a logical sequence. It all begins with an idea. This can be identified by the teacher or students, depending upon the purpose of the project. Once the idea is decided upon, it's helpful to take time to create a rubric for the final product. This approach is based on the principles of backward design, in which desired final outcomes are identified at the start of a project, decisions are made about how the outcomes will be assessed, and activities are designed that will support student success. Including students in this process helps assure buy-in right from the start of the project.

After the rubric is developed, it's time to begin mapping out the story line. When making a video, this planning often takes the form of a storyboard, which helps outline the plot and also gets students thinking about how the action will look. This is important, because students will be telling their story visually as well as through words. When the storyboard is done, it's time to develop a script. The script doesn't have to be long, but it's important to not skip this step. Even the most verbal students often find themselves tongue-tied when they have not prepared what they will say ahead of time. Writing out the dialogue and then rehearsing it will save time during the video shoot. During this phase, students also need to gather props, costumes, and any other items needed to set the stage for the video.

The next step in the process is to shoot the video. If students are well rehearsed and the video is kept short, it should be easy to complete the shoot with a minimal number of takes. Editing is one phase of video projects that can become very time consuming. To begin with, overall time requirements for completing a video project will be greatly reduced if editing is kept to a minimum. Titles and credits, some trimming, and a few transitions are probably all that's needed for a straightforward video. Music tracks and additional enhancements can be incorporated later, once students' basic skills are solid.

Finally, the video needs an audience. With whom will it be shared and how? Video files can be fairly large. Resources like *YouTube EDU* or *SchoolTube* provide storage for teacher- or student-created videos that can then be linked to a school or class website. Be sure to check your school's policies regarding posting student videos online. If use of *YouTube EDU* or *SchoolTube* is prohibited, talk with you administrators about using a local server for video storage—at least on a short term basis until some other solution can be identified. Posting videos for others to see is a critical step, because it lends authenticity to student work, demonstrating that there is an audience beyond the classroom.

VIDEO APPS

As mentioned in Chapter 2, tablets that have built-in cameras come with a preinstalled *Camera* app. To review the features of the preinstalled *Camera* app on an iPad, download the free iPad *User Guide* from the iBooks store. To learn more about the *Camera* app on a tablet running Android OS 4.1, visit *Get Help With Android,* and click on the name of your tablet type or model. Click Apps in the list of help topics that appears, and then click on Camera & Gallery. For older tablets (iPad or Android) running an earlier OS, you will need to search the Internet to find the correct user guide. Since there are several manufacturers of tablets running Windows 8, you may need to check with a specific company to get detailed camera operation information. However, a basic description for using Surface cameras is available at the support site.

In addition to the *Camera* app, tablets running iOS, Android, and Windows 8 come with a preinstalled photo gallery (called simply "Photos" on the iPad and Windows 8 tablet and "Gallery" on the Android). This is where you access videos stored on the tablet and also where it is possible to do some very basic video trimming. As is the case with the *Camera* app, the free user guides for iOS and Android described above explain how to navigate and use the photo gallery. These user guides also explain how to connect your tablet to a computer and transfer video. To learn more about photos on Windows 8 tablets, read the Andy Rathbone article (2013).

The apps mentioned above are all that's needed to get started, but teachers working with older students may want to explore alternative camera and video editing apps to meet the needs of more highly skilled students. As stated in Chapter 2, many free apps aren't as promising as they may appear to be initially, because the really nice features turn out to be in-app purchases. In other words, the basic app is free, but the effects and capabilities that make it stand apart from the preinstalled app are available only for a fee. That said, teachers may find enough features within free apps to make them worth downloading or even have a budget to cover downloading paid apps or in-app purchases.

Here are a few examples of apps that cost little or nothing and do not require in-app purchases to function. Not all are cross-platform, but there are similar apps for all three platforms.

- *YouTube Capture:* This free app runs on iOS tablets, and an Android version is expected any day. This app allows users to shoot video and upload it directly to *YouTube, Twitter, Facebook,* and/or *Google +.* A Wi-Fi connection is required for uploading, and it has minimal editing capabilities.

- *VidCam PRO:* Available for $0.99, this iOS app works on iPad 2 and later running at least iOS 6, but works best on iPad 3 and later. The app offers more control over built-in camcorder features than is available with the preinstalled camera app.
- *Camcorder Shortcut:* This is a free Android app that launches your device's default camcorder, making it easier for students to shoot video. It has no added features, just quick access to the video recording capability of the tablet.
- *CamMix:* This free app runs on Windows 8. Use the app to capture photos and video and to add special effects. Uses just one of the dual cameras.

It is possible to do some simple editing right on a tablet. Here are three apps for this purpose, one for iPad, one for Android, and one for Windows 8.

- *VidTrim–Video Trimmer:* This Android app is available in two versions, one free and one for $2.84. The free version is ad-supported. The full version is ad-free and includes all features. Use VidTrim to trim videos, convert to mp4 files, and share and play clips.
- *iMovie:* Probably the best known video editing app for iOS, iMovie costs $4.99. Use this app for on-the-spot editing of video. There are eight themes that include titles, transitions, and soundtracks.
- *Cinelab:* The free version of this Windows 8 app allows you to merge up to seven video clips into one mp4 file. You can also edit, trim, and rearrange clips. A paid in-app version is available.

STRATEGIES FOR CLASSROOM USE

Activities that incorporate video production are limited only by the teacher's imagination. Some focus on teacher-created videos designed to introduce or reinforce concepts being covered in class, while others will be student-created videos intended to demonstrate students' grasp of content or procedures. As you do with still photography, anticipate the potential for misbehavior, and use this as an opportunity to teach and model digital citizenship skills. Set expectations for student behavior and video content prior to beginning a video project. The Strategies for Classroom Use section of Chapter 2 includes a discussion of this topic that readers may want to review before continuing with this chapter.

How to best start creating video? Often, the teachers I work with prefer to increase their own level of comfort with video production by making their own videos before asking students to create videos. This approach familiarizes teachers with the mechanics of video production. It also encourages them to extend their reach with students and parents by sharing the videos they record. For example, after introducing a complex concept in class, teachers prepare a short video recapping the key points of the concept, or reviewing steps for completing a related task, and post it on the class web page for students and parents to view. Or, they record a brief (5 minutes or less) video tutorial explaining the procedure for a regularly required task, such as using a web-based collaboration tool or citing references in a bibliography.

Producing three- to five-minute videos for student or parent audiences is labor intensive at first, but there are good reasons to do it. A recent review of literature related to use of video in the classroom finds that viewing instructional video can lead to positive results in a lengthy list of areas, including grades, school readiness, workforce preparation, academic growth overall, ability to work collaboratively, and more (Greenberg & Zanetis, 2012). Growing numbers of teachers who regularly use the "flipped classroom" instructional strategy recommend that colleagues create their own video instead of relying on video from an outside source. This is because locally developed videos directly address student needs, while video created by someone else may or may not provide targeted assistance to students.

When is the best time to use teacher-created video? Teachers must exercise professional judgment about when and how to best use video to introduce and/or reinforce concepts. The important thing to keep in mind is that students need to be active, not passive, viewers of the material. Students can learn from watching video, but pedagogy matters (Bossewitch & Preston, 2011). KQED Public Media for Northern California offers a free guide entitled *Tools and Techniques for Using Spark in the Classroom*. Although this guide is written for a specific video production program, Spark, the engagement strategies described for use before, during, and after a video is shown in a classroom are applicable to any viewing experience. They include suggestions like using K-W-L charts for pre- and postassessment of student knowledge, giving students a task to complete while viewing, or repeating viewing to encourage deeper understanding of the material.

Video production lends itself very well to small group work. It's natural to identify individual roles like those of cameraperson, director, scriptwriter, and actor, so that each group member has one or more responsibilities. As mentioned in the chapter on still photography, this is a time when one-to-one access to tablets isn't required or even necessarily desirable. Each group will need one tablet with a video-capable camera. Storyboarding might be accomplished more efficiently offline, depending on students' capabilities and the format of the storyboard template. And scriptwriting can be done using a laptop, desktop, or tablet depending upon access and personal preference. Regardless of the technologies used, build frequent benchmarks into the group's work, so it's easy to monitor progress.

Teachers will need to decide ahead of time how complex the video will be. Keep it simple, at least initially—one to three minutes is a good length to start with. Production values can be impacted by location. Students can practice in the classroom, but when it's time to record, they need a location that is fairly quiet and well lit and that does not have a lot of foot traffic (where passersby can become background distractions). Since students will likely be using the built-in microphone, sound checks are important before shooting. Actors will need to adjust their speaking volume based on the results of the audio checks. Lighting can also be problematic, so it's a good idea to shoot some test footage to ensure that there is neither glare nor a distracting shadow. It's not always easy to adjust lighting in a school setting, but basic tricks like having windows at the back of the camera person or turning off some or all overhead lights can be very helpful.

Decide how much editing is needed or desirable. With a short video, it may be more efficient to reshoot than edit out mistakes. Some teachers have students do basic editing right on the tablet, using a video-editing app. Others have students transfer the video file to a laptop or desktop computer before editing. When editing on a tablet, it may be easier if the tablet screen is projected onto a larger screen to enlarge the image and facilitate clip trimming.

Small group video production relies heavily on students' abilities to work collaboratively. Successful cooperative learning is discussed in the section Strategies for Classroom Use of Chapter 2. Readers may want to refer back to that chapter.

ACTIVITY SUGGESTIONS

Videos captured with tablet devices can be used to meet virtually any standard performance indicator in any content area. Once teachers and students are comfortable with basic operation of the camera app being used, it's time to develop and produce videos that present information or demonstrate learning. Even very young children can participate in video production. It may be best to engage these students in class projects, but I have worked with preschool teachers whose four- and five-year-old students have created simple videos. Planned activities need to be based on meaningful teaching and learning. Here are some ideas that can be used by teachers and students.

Model desired behaviors: Special education teachers have known for a long time that children with developmental disabilities can learn appropriate behaviors through video modeling (Dana, n.d.). But the power of video modeling isn't limited to this student population. Anyone who has observed children watching video programs knows that they often mimic the behaviors they are watching, both while they are viewing and later.

Teachers can develop scripts that target a specific desired behavior and then make a video of themselves or students modeling the behavior. For example, preschool teachers save time at the start of the school year by making videos of classroom procedures like folding a nap blanket or cleaning up the block center. Once the teacher has modeled a behavior in the classroom with children, the students can review the steps by watching the video at school during center time or at home. This idea works well throughout grade levels.

Students can also create videos of their own that model appropriate behaviors. A high school teacher had her life skills students create a series of videos modeling how to apply for a job, from submitting an application through sending a postinterview thank-you note. Not only did this provide an opportunity for students to demonstrate their understanding of these critical workplace skills, but it also resulted in a video series that can be shared with students in years to come.

One-minute video: Published in 2004, *Classroom Instruction That Works: Research-Based Strategies for Increasing Student Achievement* (Marzano, Pickering, & Pollack, 2004) identifies nine instructional strategies that are particularly effective in classrooms. One of these strategies is summarizing. One of these strategies is one-minute videos, which challenge students to present a concept or information about a topic in just one minute. This assignment taps higher order thinking skills, because students are asked to identify information that is essential to share and then put it into their own words. Sample one-minute book reviews can be accessed on the SchoolTube website; type "book reviews" in the search box to access a list of reviews posted by a variety of students.

An extension for this activity is to have students share their summaries through mock commercials or public service announcements. This provides a structure that may be more interesting than a simple overview, and it challenges students to "sell" their ideas. Students will require more support for this modified activity but will also have more opportunity to explore their creativity.

Tutorial: Tutorials differ from modeling videos in that they show how to complete a task rather than model a social skill. Teachers who create and share video tutorials for students provide a real service to both their pupils and their pupils' families. So often students will appear to grasp material covered in class, only to find when they get home that confusion reigns. If the classroom teacher has posted a short tutorial on the material, the student will be able to review the video and have a much better chance of completing homework correctly.

Even more important, student-created tutorials can serve two valuable purposes. First, when students script and record a tutorial, they are thinking out loud. This can be a great diagnostic tool for teachers to review for the student's level of understanding of a concept. Second, teaching a skill or concept to someone else is an excellent way for the student doing the teaching to also master the material (Jackel, 2008). And, the resulting tutorial can be added to a repository of student-created tutorials that can be shared with other students.

In addition to using the video recording capabilities of the built-in camera, owners of iOS or Android devices can create video tutorials using a free screencasting app such as *ScreenChomp* or *Educreations* for iOS or a low-cost app like *Explain Everything* for iOS and Android. A more in-depth discussion of screencasting is found in Chapter 7, but basically, these apps provide a whiteboard background students can use to write or draw on while recording an audio explanation. It's also possible to import photos or other images to use as a background. Each of the apps mentioned here allows users to record with or without a Wi-Fi connection and then upload the video when the iPad connects to a network. Tablets running the full version of Windows 8 are able to use free screencasting tools like *Jing* or *Screenr*, but tablets running RT cannot, because they cannot run Java. A recently released *TechSmith* app called *Ask3* enables teachers and students to sign up for free class space, then record shared videos that can be responded to online using text or another video.

Show what you know: The video projects suggested so far are based on teachers and students confining their videos to topics covered in class. However, educators and students know a lot about subjects that may not be included in the curriculum. Show-what-you-know videos offer opportunities for adults and students to demonstrate real-life skills that may (or may not) be covered in the curriculum. Teachers can share their personal interests or demonstrate ties between classroom activities and the real world and learn more about their students by asking them to create videos about their knowledge related to activities outside the school day.

This chapter covers just a few of the ways that tablet cameras can be used to create instructional content. To learn more, review the entries in the resources section below. You may also find it helpful to review and talk about the discussion points provided here.

Discussion Points

1. How do you use digital video personally? Which uses are most important to you and why?

2. Create a list of topics for tutorial videos teachers and students in your school or district could create and post.

3. Review student- and teacher-created videos posted on *YouTube EDU*, *SchoolTube*, or another video site where this type of video is posted. Describe the kinds of videos you find. Would you be interested in replicating any of the projects you find? Why, or why not?

4. Choose one of the activities suggested in this chapter. Develop a lesson plan for the activity that you can use with students.

REFERENCES AND ADDITIONAL RESOURCES

Apps and reports/articles mentioned in this chapter are listed here, as are additional resources that offer further information about topics discussed in this chapter.

Apps

Ask3. http://bit.ly/TZMBHg
CamCorder Shortcut. http://www.dexati.com/android.html
CamMix. http://goo.gl/X7KIfu
Cinelab. http://goo.gl/3VBNcX
Educreations. http://bit.ly/Z6hAli
Explain Everything. http://www.explaineverything.com/
iMovie. http://bit.ly/TZSSCY
Jing. http://www.techsmith.com/jing.html
ScreenChomp. http://bit.ly/Z6hjPp
Screenr. http://www.screenr.com
VidCam PRO. http://bit.ly/TZU6hs
VidTrim—Video Trimmer. http://bit.ly/TZTVCO
YouTube Capture. http://bit.ly/TZTmc5

Books

Marzano, R., Pickering, D., & Pollack, J. (2004). *Classroom instruction that works: Research-based strategies for increasing student achievement*. Alexandria, VA: Pearson.

Websites

Get Help With Android. http://bit.ly/TV5Dfm.
SchoolTube. http://www.schooltube.com/
Surface Cameras. http://goo.gl/9txrF
TechSmith. http://www.techsmith.com
WatchKnowLearn. http://www.watchknowlearn.org/
YouTube EDU. http://www.youtube.com/education

Online Reports and Articles

Backward design. (2012, November). In *Wikipedia*. Retrieved from http://en.wikipedia.org/wiki/Backward_design

Bossewitch, J., & Preston, M. (2011, March). *Teaching and learning with video annotations.* Learning Through Digital Media Experiments in Technology and Pedagogy. Retrieved from http://learningthroughdigitalmedia.net/teaching-and-learning-with-video-annotations

Cradler, J., Freeman, M., & Cradler, R. (2005). *Research basis for the Schlessinger media programs grades K–12.* Educational Support Systems, Inc. Retrieved from http://www.bcps.org/offices/lis/safari/Cradlerpaper62105_32_June22[1].pdf

Cruse, E. (2009). *Using educational video in the classroom: Theory, research and practice.* Library Video Company. Retrieved from http://www.safarimontage.com/pdfs/training/UsingEducationalVideoInTheClassroom.pdf

Dana, T. (n.d.). *Using video to teach social skills.* Retrieved from http://tdsocialskills.com/using_video_to_teach_social_skil.htm

Greenberg, A., & Zanetis, J. (2012, March). *The impact of broadcast and streaming video in education.* Wainhouse Research. Retrieved from http://www.cisco.com/web/strategy/docs/education/ciscovideowp.pdf

Jackel, M. (2008, June). Wisdom of the (multi) ages: Students Learn by teaching. *Edutopia.* Retrieved from http://bit.ly/TZMBHg

Marshall, J. (2002, May). *Learning with technology: Evidence that technology can, and does, support learning.* San Diego State University. Retrieved from http://www.medialit.org/reading-room/learning-technology

Marzano's nine instructional strategies for effective teaching and learning. (n.d.). Retrieved from http://bit.ly/rME88a

Overbaugh, R., & Schultz, L. (n.d.) *Bloom's Taxonomy.* Old Dominion University. Retrieved from http://ww2.odu.edu/educ/roverbau/Bloom/blooms_taxonomy.htm

Rathbone, A. (2013). How to view photos on your Windows 8 tablet. *Windows for Tablets for Dummies.* Retrieved from http://goo.gl/HLUZq

Rusen, C. A. (2013, February 27). *Introducing Windows 8: How to use the camera app to record videos.* Retrieved from http://goo.gl/aEI1e

Stokes, K. (2012, June). *Why good teachers—not good videos—are key to the flipped classroom.* StateImpact. Retrieved from http://bit.ly/14ZF4vD

Tools and techniques for using spark in the classroom. (n.d.). Spark in Education, KQED.org. Retrieved from http://www.kqed.org/assets/pdf/arts/programs/spark/video.pdf

Watching videos can help children with autism learn social skills. (2007, March). Indiana Resource Center for Autism. Retrieved from http://newsinfo.iu.edu/web/page/normal/5254.html

Wright, J. C., Huston, A. C., Murphy, K. C., St. Peters, M., Pinon, M., Scantlin, R., & Kotler, J. (2001, September/October). The relations of early television viewing to school readiness and vocabulary of children from low-income families: The early window project. *Child Development, 72*(5), 1347–1366.

Using Tablets to Enhance Speaking and Listening

W e know that the three Rs include reading, 'riting, and 'rithmetic—the skills that have historically been paid the greatest attention in K–12 education. But there are additional foundational capabilities students must develop to master academic content. Two of these fundamental skills, the ability to speak and to listen, are actually two of the four pillars of effective language arts programs identified in content standards documents for decades. In fact, there is discussion in Common Core State Standards materials about the critical role speaking and listening skills play in students' ability to read and write, where it is pointed out that good readers must first be good listeners, and good writers' skills are the result of good speaking skills. In societies where visual media regularly supersede audio media, students have fewer opportunities to learn how to listen and speak well.

Fortunately, tablet devices are tools both teachers and students can use to address these two important skills. This chapter explores several ways teachers and their students can use tablet devices to make and use audio content.

LISTENING AND SPEAKING—SKILLS FOR LIFE

Visual literacy is an essential modern skill set. In fact, it may sometimes appear that the ability to read and understand visual cues provided through text, images, and other media trumps other literacy skills. But much communication—both formal and informal—relies on the ability to speak and to listen. Research in the teaching of listening and speaking skills indicates that these should be taught beginning in preschool, and then on through Grade 12 and even into postsecondary education. Jack C. Richards (2008) writes that instruction in listening needs to include not just skills for comprehension—understanding what's being said—but also skills for acquisition—listening to increase personal vocabulary and use of language conventions. Richards suggests that there are three broad classes of speaking—interactions, transactions, and performances—each with its own skill set. Social interactions require facility in the first of these, interactions, engaging in the give and take of conversation, knowing when to speak and when to listen. But many classroom activities still focus only on the latter two—teachers and students conduct verbal transactions where information is exchanged and discussed, and activities such as lectures or oral reports are designed for performance purposes.

Think about the structure of classrooms on your site or within your district. How much of the time are students expected to listen or to speak? How difficult is it for them to attend on these occasions? How much time is spent in direct instruction designed to help students strengthen skills in these areas? These are critical questions to ask when the student population consists of native English speakers who are performing at or above grade level. But how many classrooms serve students who speak other primary languages, or who struggle academically? These students need even more support with development of speaking and listening skills.

Another concern is that direct instruction in speaking and listening skills may be provided most often for younger students and then decrease during middle grades or high school, except for those students enrolled in elective courses such as Speech or Drama. This is problematic, because when employers are asked to identify workplace skills they expect new hires to have, oral communication skills fall in the top five regardless of the new employee's level of education— high school diploma, two-year degree, or four-year degree (Casner-Lotto, Barrington, & Wright, 2006). And so, although visual literacy skills are important, those students who are adept at speaking and listening will more readily find success in the workplace than those who lack these skills.

How have these activities been structured tradition- ally? Beginning with the youngest of students, exercises that incorporate songs, poetry, show-and-tell, reading aloud, and similar undertakings address speaking and listening skills. Interestingly, technologies of various types—tape recorders or record players—have often been used to support many of these activities. As children grow older, they are still encour- aged to read aloud and make classroom presentations, but there may be less direct instruction in how to improve these skills and a higher expectation that students already know how to speak and listen. Yet another factor in the lack of instruction in these skills may be that it is more difficult to accurately assess speaking and listening skills in a standard- ized test than it is to measure skills in reading and writing. And with the focus that has been place on standardized test scores for a number of years now, educators' attention has focused on what's covered in the test.

It may be difficult to directly assess speaking and listen- ing in a high-stakes test, but increasing students' skills in speaking and listening can help them raise their achieve- ment test scores. For example, students who know how to listen to directions, who can ask the right questions, and who have increased their vocabularies through oral language acquisition activities will have an advantage over students whose skills in these areas are weak. Another advantage of technology-supported activities focused on these areas is that educators can extend their personal outreach to individual students and lengthen the school day through use of audio-based activities. Any additional time students spend engaged in activities based in academics will help them learn.

As is the case with photography and video, audio projects can quickly become unwieldy. Keep the focus on the learning objective(s), and keep the activity simple, particularly at the outset. As your skills and those of your students increase, it's always possible to add embellishments using a free audio editing tool like *Audacity.*

AUDIO RECORDING BASICS

The Strategies for Classroom Use section of this chapter discusses various kinds of audio recordings students and teachers might want to make. This section covers the basics for making simple audio recordings that enable students to practice both their speaking and listening skills.

Making a simple audio recording requires a tablet and an app. (See the next section of this chapter for a discussion of apps for recording audio.) Tablets do have a built-in microphone, and audio recordings can be made using this; however, background noise is often a problem in classrooms. Some teachers address this problem by building a small sound booth—not a realistic option for everyone. An alternative solution is to purchase and use earbuds that have a built-in microphone. Reasonably priced third-party options are available online. This is an effective remedy when recording just one person's voice at a time. To capture audio from a group, there are external microphones that interface with iOS, Android, and Windows 8 devices. Available online or at electronics stores, external microphones range in price from less than $50 to $199 or more. To determine the best configuration for your classroom, start with the built-in microphone, and see what happens. Then, depending upon those results, add earbuds with a microphone or an external microphone.

Commercial audio recordings run anywhere from just a couple of minutes in length to several hours long in the case of audiobooks. For classroom activities, it's best to begin with fairly brief technology-supported activities for speaking and listening and then expand them as students' skills increase. To start with, making or listening to recordings of three to five minutes will be sufficient.

Designing and making a simple audio recording is similar to planning and recording an instructional video. Here is the list of basic steps:

1. Identify ideas related to the assignment topic, and select one (may be identified by the teacher or by students).

2. Create a rubric for the final product to identify and describe desired outcomes.

3. Outline the contents of the recording. This could be a mind map or flowchart.

4. Develop a script to use as a guide while recording.

5. Rehearse the script several times to facilitate recording.

6. Think about sound effects. If these are required, what will be used to create the sound(s)? Gather any materials needed.

7. Record the audio in one take if possible. This reduces or eliminates the need for anything other than basic editing.

8. Additional tracks and other enhancements can be incorporated later, once students master basic skills.

Finally, the recordings need an audience. Depending upon the subject and purpose of the audio, decide with whom will it be shared and how. There are many online file storage services. Well known options include *Dropbox, Box,* and *SkyDrive,* and there are others as well. Research them to choose the best for your situation.

APPS FOR RECORDING AUDIO

A voice memo app came preinstalled on some early generations of iPod Touches and iPhones. In order to make audio recordings on later models of iOS devices and other types of mobile technologies, a free or low-cost app must be downloaded. There are many to choose from. On the iOS side, try the free version of *iTalk,* an iPhone app that works on iPod Touches, iPads, and iPhones. For Android tablets, check out a free app called *Easy Voice Recorder,* and Windows 8 tablet users can try the free *Dictaphone* app. Apps for recording audio can be used for a variety of purposes, from making a podcast to helping students self-assess their reading fluency.

Simple voice recorders only scratch the surface of audio recording with tablets. For example, it's possible to compose and record music, make voice-to-text recordings that render speech into print, and even embellish basic audio recording and improve study skills by annotating audio recordings of meetings or class lectures.

Here are some examples of apps that are inexpensive or free that can be used for the purposes mentioned above. Not all are cross-platform, but there are similar apps for both platforms.

- *iTalk:* This free iOS phone app runs on tablets as well. It's a basic audio recorder. Open the app, select recording quality, tap the red button to start recording, and tap again to stop. Once the recording is saved, give it a title, and then add to it or e-mail it to yourself to easily transfer to a laptop. Recordings are saved on the device until deleted.
- *Easy Voice Recorder:* This is the free Android app equivalent of *iTalk.*
- *Dictaphone:* This is the free Windows 8 app equivalent of *iTalk.*
- *GarageBand:* This robust app ($4.99) gives users a mobile recording studio. In addition to voice recording,

GarageBand supports eight-track recording and smart instruments for music composition.

- *PocketBand Pro:* This Android app costs $9.99, but there is a free lite version you can test-drive. The app includes a 12-channel mixer, drum machine, recorder, and more.

- *Recording Studio:* This free Windows 8 app is designed to facilitate recording, editing, and mixing. The free version supports two tracks and one virtual instrument. The pro version ($7.99) supports 24 tracks and seven virtual instruments.

- *Dragon Dictation:* A free iOS app for iPad 1 and 2 that supports voice-to-text dictation. It takes practice to "train" the app to recognize your voice, but this is great for helping students improve enunciation. The app requires a wireless connection to render voice input to text. You do not need this app for Windows 8 and Android devices or for iPad 3 and later, as these devices support voice-to-text in virtually any app that accepts text input.

- *AudioNote:* Available for $4.99, this app works on iOS and Android tablets. There is a Windows software download that works on tablets running full Windows 8. Use it to make an audio recording of a lecture or meeting, and add annotations as you record to make it easy to access and listen to specific portions of the recording. Adding annotations provides good practice in deciding what's important. The free version supports 10-minute recording; the paid version supports lengthy recordings.

There are other apps that support audio recording. Some are designed to help users create narrated storybooks, others to make audio flashcards and more. To find apps like these, conduct an Internet search using keywords that include "audio recording," "iOS app," "Android app," "Windows 8 app," and/or "storytelling app."

STRATEGIES FOR CLASSROOM USE

As is the case with video and photography, educators can use audio recording to support instruction in virtually any content area. The key to success with these ventures is determining which skills for speaking and listening will be targeted within the context of working on academic material. (Refer back to the research cited earlier in this chapter.) In a particular instance, would students benefit most from listening for comprehension or for acquisition? Which type of speaking activity would be most effective within the context of the content being covered? Would it be most effective to ask students to focus on speaking to interact, transact, or present? It is also important to decide when it's most appropriate for audio material to be teacher-created and when students need to take the lead.

How to best start working with audio-based activities? Using a tablet as a recording device is new, but the basic principles for making a recording are familiar to most of us, so teachers should feel comfortable making their own. What may be a bit different is thinking about how to design activities for students based upon the purpose for the speaking and/ or listening students will be expected to do, along with how audio files might be embellished using a tablet. This approach encourages teachers to extend their reach with students by offering audio activities that are completed in class or posted online for use outside the regular school day. For example, teachers prepare and post lesson summaries that students listen to in order to check their understanding of material presented during class. These same audio summaries are helpful to parents who need to quickly brush up on a topic before working at home with their children. The primary purpose for listening in this case is comprehension. Or, record text that students listen to and make use of as they complete offline activities that require them to develop language awareness. These activities include identifying expressions used in the text or comparing a print version of the text to the recording to identify differences. In these instances, the primary objective for listening is acquisition.

Recording audio files for use at school and off campus takes time initially. However, once recorded, these files lay the foundation for a library of audio files that are stored online and available to parents and students on demand. That said, teachers do not need to be responsible for making all the recordings used for instruction. It's true that being a good listener is an important skill, but it's equally true that speaking is a critical skill to develop. Research shows that when learners speak, they are also developing thinking skills, but educators tend to speak far more often in classrooms than do their students (Hudson, 2007). Recruiting students to record audio files for classroom use provides opportunities for them to think not just about listening, but also about speaking.

What kinds of audio-based activities work well with students? It might be easier to identify what doesn't work well than to try to cover all the listening and speaking activities that students enjoy and benefit from. An obvious positive choice is the listening center, which can be designed to serve everyone, from the very youngest of students—through read-aloud books, music, and chants—to high school students who are learning a foreign language or listening to full-length audio books. Students also benefit from listening to themselves speak or read—an activity that helps them gauge their own fluency or articulation skills. Recordings of Readers Theater productions or short podcasts about virtually any topic provide practice in both skill areas.

Audio production does not need to be limited to recording speech. Tablets offer additional capabilities that provide practice in speaking and/or listening but with different end products. For example, Windows 8 and Android devices as well as iPad 3s and later offer built-in voice-to-text capability in any app that accepts typed text. This means that teachers and students can dictate something, and the mobile device will render the speech into text. This feature requires a Wi-Fi connection for iOS and Android (but not for Windows 8) and works better when the speaker has earbuds with a built-in microphone to reduce background noise. On iOS devices, the user dictates for about 30 seconds, and then waits for the text to be rendered before being able to read it. On Windows 8 and Android devices, the text appears as it is spoken. All three operating systems support easy editing and saving of text once it is rendered.

Using voice-to-text requires practice. The speaker must enunciate clearly in order for the text to be rendered accurately, and the software does not always deal well with heavily accented English. By the same token, it can be a great way to help students improve the clarity of their speech and is a real boon to those whose typing skills are limited for whatever reason. There is a free app called *Dragon Dictation* that supports voice-to-text on iPad 1 and 2, but all dictation must be done within the app and then copied and pasted into another app or e-mailed from within the app to be used elsewhere.

Another recording capability teachers may want to explore is the ability to compose and save music on a tablet. iPads can run a mobile version of *GarageBand* ($4.99), and there are equivalent Android apps such as *PocketBand Pro* ($9.99) and Windows 8 apps like *Recording Studio* (free, pro version available for $7.99). Many educators argue that music instruction results in a myriad of benefits for students, including improved critical thinking and listening skills (Brown, n.d.).

With the exception of voice-to-text, other audio recording can be subjected to as much editing as the teacher deems necessary. If students practice whatever they are saying prior to recording, they may be able to speak their pieces without any major mistakes. If a recording is not interesting to listen to, the issue is more likely a need for vocal expression or variety than a need for a music track. There are apps that support basic editing on the tablet, but more can be done if the file is transferred to a computer and edited using a free program like *Audacity*.

As is the case with video production and photography, small group audio recording relies heavily on students' abilities to work collaboratively. Successful cooperative learning is discussed in the Strategies for Classroom Use section of Chapter 2. Readers may want to refer back to that chapter.

ACTIVITY SUGGESTIONS

Audio recordings made or played using tablet devices can meet virtually any standard performance indicator depending on the content of the recording and how the activity is structured. Even the most basic app will require a little orientation, while voice-to-text, music composition, and note-taking apps will require more direct instruction in their use. Once app basics are mastered, it's time to get creative. Remember that, in addition to the academic content being covered, audio recordings can also be used to target specific skills in listening and speaking. Students of all ages can create and use audio recordings. Audio production projects work best when set up for small groups, with the exception of voice-to-text and note-taking, which tend to work better for individuals. Whole-class projects work well with very young children with many types of audio recordings and musical composition. Remember that many of these projects can serve a dual purpose. First, speaking skills can be addressed as recordings are made, and then listening skills as students use recordings made by their classmates. Here are some ideas that can be used by teachers and students.

Podcasts: Wikipedia defines *podcast* as follows:

a type of digital media consisting of an episodic series of audio radio, video, pdf, or epub files subscribed to and downloaded through web syndication or streamed online to a computer or mobile device. The word is a neologism derived from "broadcast" and "pod" from the success of the iPod, as podcasts are often listened to on portable media players. ("Podcast," 2013)

For the purposes of discussion here, *podcast* refers to audio radio recordings.

Podcasts emerged as an entertainment form in the early 2000s, coinciding with the production of MP3 players that made it easy to download and listen to audio programs on these mobile devices. Podcasts can run anywhere from a few minutes to an hour or more in length. Much like radio programs, podcast content ranges from music to talk shows to scripted performances. End users subscribe to podcasts, which can be automatically downloaded to a portable device, including a tablet, using whatever method of synchronizing is available for that device.

It didn't take long for inventive educators to start recording podcast programs for their own classes or even their whole schools. The target audience typically includes other students, parents, and members of the community at large. Content includes everything from information being covered in class to student performances and school news. While greater access to digital cameras that record video has decreased the popularity of podcasts to a degree, the importance of use of audio files cannot be overstressed. Video can make it too easy for creators to show something instead of relying on use of language to describe something, cheating themselves and their audience of opportunities to practice critical skills.

Consider balanced use of visual and audio media. Visual literacy is important, but so is the ability to listen carefully and speak well. Podcasts do not need to be complicated in order to be useful. As mentioned earlier in this chapter, teachers often create and post brief podcasts that summarize material covered in class that students can use to get caught up when they've been absent or as a study tool when preparing for an exam. Student-created podcasts might consist of a brief school news program with regular segments contributed by small groups, explanations of content covered in class (rules of grammar and book reviews are popular topics), or scripted programs such as a radio play, recitations, or songs. The critical thing with podcasting is that it implies regularity, so make a time commitment that can be kept—weekly, monthly, quarterly—and then live up to that commitment. Then make recordings easily accessible through a school web page or app store appropriate for the devices being used.

Read-Along Books: Audio books have long been popular in listening centers. Beginning with storybooks for very young children and then chapter books for older students, teachers have extended their reach with students by providing recorded books students can listen to while following along with a print copy. Often these are professionally produced, but they don't have to be. Teachers and students who are readers can make recordings of books for other students to listen to. All you need in addition to the hardware and app for recording is a book and, for younger students, a bell or other noisemaker to indicate when it's time to turn the page.

Making your own read-along books is an excellent way to model expressive oral reading, and it is also a great way for student readers to work on their own fluency and articulation. It may take several tries for students to come up with a recording they are satisfied with, but this is time well spent on a number of levels. While these recordings can be planned and completed individually, working in small groups provides opportunities to enhance collaboration skills as well as speaking and listening skills.

This activity can easily be extended to readings beyond books for a listening center. For students who are learning English as a second language, who are learning another language, or who need to work on articulation in any language, it is very helpful to record themselves when they read aloud, so they can listen to what they sound like afterward. The ability to hear themselves as others hear them is a valuable tool for self-assessment and improvement.

Voice-to-Text: This strategy tends to be individual in nature, although students can work in pairs or trios on a common assignment, taking turns dictating their text. The value in using voice-to-text is twofold. First, students must speak clearly for the app to accurately render their speech into text. While it is not appropriate to ask a student with a severe speech impediment or who speaks heavily accented English to use voice-to-text, it is an excellent tool for students who are fairly articulate but need practice in speaking more clearly. Second, and especially for students who are well spoken, it is an opportunity for students to focus on punctuation and grammar, because they are able to include commands in their dictation that will be rendered along with the text. So, for example, they can add punctuation marks or tell the software to begin a new paragraph. It does take practice, but it is a real time saver for students who master this interesting capability of tablets.

Even more important, student-created tutorials can serve two valuable purposes. First, when students script and record a tutorial, they are thinking out loud. This is a great diagnostic tool for teachers to use to review a student's level of understanding of a concept. Second, teaching a skill or concept to someone else is an excellent way for the student doing the teaching to also master the material (Jackel, 2008). Add the resulting tutorial to a repository of student-created tutorials to share with other students. Remember, there must be a Wi-Fi connection for the voice-to-text feature to work (except with Windows 8), but when there is, it's great for lab notes and field notes as well as for students with limited typing skills.

Note taking: This is a strategy best used individually with older students, but sharing notes with one another is an option for students who have the *AudioNote* app installed on their tablets.

Taking notes in class is an ongoing challenge for students who tend to either overwrite or miss the important points of a lecture or discussion, because they don't know how to listen discriminately. An app like *AudioNote* makes it possible for students to make an annotated audio recording of class activity. It's simple to use and helps students learn to identify important points to mark for later reference. All that's required is to open the app and tap the button to begin the recording. A blank note page is provided. Every time the student begins a new note, which can be typed, handwritten, or drawn, the recording is bookmarked. When the recording is completed, it can be saved for later listening or shared with another device that has the app installed. There is also a way to share the audio and a time-stamped transcript of notes with someone who doesn't have the app, but the link between the audio and the notes is lost in the process.

This chapter covers several ways that tablets can be used to create audio content that is instructional. To learn more, review the entries in the resources section below. You may also find it helpful to review and talk about the discussion points provided here.

Discussion Points

1. Have you subscribed to a podcast or listened to one? If so, what personal benefits have you derived from this practice, and if not, why not?

2. Brainstorm a list of books that teachers and students in your school or district could record for read-aloud activities.

3. Think about ways students in your school or district could use voice-to-text to improve articulation and save time when writing. Try dictating some text yourself. Be sure to include punctuation and/or commands like "new paragraph." How well does voice-to-text work for you? Would this be a tablet feature your students could use? Why, or why not?

4. How well do your students take notes? Would an app like *AudioNote* be useful for them? Download the free lite version and give it a try. What do you think, and why?

REFERENCES AND ADDITIONAL RESOURCES

Apps and reports/articles mentioned in this chapter are listed here, as are additional resources that offer further information about topics discussed in this chapter.

Apps and Tools

Audacity. http://audacity.sourceforge.net/
AudioNote. http://luminantsoftware.com/iphone/

audionote.html

Box. http://www.box.com

Dictaphone. http://goo.gl/44dAZ

Dragon Dictation. http://bit.ly/W6tacw

Dropbox. http://www.dropbox.com

Easy Voice Recorder. http://bit.ly/W6thVu

GarageBand. http://bit.ly/W6tjg2

iTalk Recorder. http://bit.ly/QJU6fc

PocketBand Pro. http://bit.ly/W6ttUH

Recording Studio. http://goo.gl/GSgeX

SkyDrive. http://skydrive.live.com/

Online Reports and Articles

Brown, L. (n.d.) *The benefits of music education.* PBS Parents. Retrieved from http://www.pbs.org/parents/education/music-arts/the-benefits-of-music-education/

Casner-Lotto, J., Barrington, L., & Wright, M. (2006). *Are they really ready to work?* The Partnership for 21st Century Skills in collaboration with The Conference Board, Corporate Voices for Working Families, and The Society for Human Resource Management. Retrieved from http://www.p21.org/storage/documents/FINAL_REPORT_PDF09-29-06.pdf

Developing listening and speaking skills. (2002). Excerpt from Teaching our Youngest. Head Start Early Childhood Learning & Knowledge Center. Retrieved from http://goo.gl/PDoSa

Hudson, C. (2007). *Improving speaking and listening skills.* Annesley, Nottingham, UK: DFES Publications. Retrieved from https://www.education.gov.uk/publications/eOrderingDownload/SandLPACK02.pdf

Jackel, M. (2008, June). Wisdom of the (multi) ages: Students learn by teaching. *Edutopia.* Retrieved from http://bit.ly/TZMBHg

Listening and speaking activities—Grade 8. (n.d.). Columbus, OH: Glencoe McGraw-Hill. Retrieved from http://bit.ly/W6tFU8

Listening and speaking: Background information & activities. (n.d.). BrainPOP Jr. Retrieved http://bit.ly/W6tCYh

Podcast. (2013). In *Wikipedia.* Retrieved from http://en.wikipedia.org/wiki/Podcast

Richards, J. C. (2008). *Teaching listening and speaking: From theory to practice.* New York, NY: Cambridge University Press. Retrieved from http://www.cambridge.org/other_files/downloads/esl/booklets/Richards-Teaching-Listening-Speaking.pdf

5

Student Authors

Compose and Publish

Second-grade students are investigating growth of potted plants in the classroom by making observations, describing what they see, and recording measurements. They work in small groups to gather and record data—notes and photos— using a tablet device. Records are uploaded to the cloud, where they are saved in a common folder. At the end of the children's study, their notes and photos will be merged into a pdf file and published as a class e-book to place in the class e-library and share with other students and parents.

Seventh-grade students are writing and illustrating essays describing real events. Each essay includes links to supporting resources found online. The text is written using laptops or tablets, depending on student preference. Illustrations can be photographs or digital drawings or paintings created using a tablet. Once an essay is written and edited by a peer, the author uses a tool like *FlipSnack* to publish and share the illustrated essay as a "flipping book."

High school students are using blogs to tackle character analysis as they read Shakespeare's *Julius Caesar*. Groups of five or six students are multiauthoring blogs; each student is assigned one character from the play. They write original blogs posts and reply to others, but all writing must be in their character's voice. This ongoing assignment wraps up when the play is finished—in the meantime, each student is expected to post and reply more than once every day. At the conclusion of the assignment, the blogs are closed to new posts, and comments and the links are posted in a class archive for public viewing.

The students described above think of themselves as writers. What about your students? Do they appreciate the value of expressing thoughts using the written word? We say that the foundation of a good education is grounded in the three Rs—reading, 'riting, and 'rithmetic—but do we devote as much time to teaching writing as we do to reading and mathematics? Students frequently balk at daily writing assignments—e-publishing in various forms is a fun way to involve them in regularly writing, publishing, and distributing their work.

This approach to creating content is a bit different from other techniques described in this book. More than other forms of content creation, e-publishing works best when using a blend of tablets and computers. In addition, the importance of student writing in overall academic growth cannot be overemphasized. As a result, this chapter spends a bit of time discussing the academic rationale for getting students to write as often as possible before moving into an overview of e-publishing and ways teachers and students can use tablets and other technologies to increase the amount of writing they do, both informally and formally. The chapter also describes strategies young authors can use to seek peer feedback on their writing and publish their work for audiences beyond the walls of the classroom.

THE CASE FOR STUDENT WRITING

The writing study group of the NCTE Executive Committee (2004) suggests that writing plays a critical role in students' overall academic preparation. The group stresses that both informal and formal writing are necessary and should be incorporated into every school day. The Common Core State Standards (CCSS) set a high bar for K–12 students when it comes to skills in composition. Students are expected to develop their writing abilities across all disciplines as well as in various fiction and nonfiction genres, including narrative, informational, argument, and more. In order to achieve these goals, students need to write daily.

It's important to allow students to express themselves through personal writing, but it's equally—and some would argue even more—important to teach the mechanics of good writing. Correct grammar and punctuation, proper spelling, and coherent organization are all critical as students hone written communication skills that will serve them not only in academic life but in adulthood as well. Sherrelle Walker, a regular contributor to The Science of Learning Blog, explains there are five reasons students of all ages need to engage in writing activities on a daily basis. Here is a summary of her list. Students can use writing to

1. Improve their skills in communication and expression.

2. Help themselves remember something they've just learned.

3. Demonstrate their understanding of a concept.

4. Explore language and express their ideas creatively, both formally and informally.

5. Develop self-understanding through reflection. (Walker, 2012)

Granted, it's difficult for a teacher who regularly works with one class of students to read everything they write every day, and it's impossible for teachers who meet with five or six different groups every day to keep up with everything all their students write. But that doesn't mean that students shouldn't be writing regularly. It means that strategies employed for monitoring and grading of that writing need to be modified so that the teacher is not overwhelmed. The article *Responding to Writing: Contexts and Strategies* (2004) found in the References and Additional Resources section at the end of this chapter suggests several practical tactics secondary teachers can use to reduce their grading workload and keep students writing regularly. Elementary teachers may want to check out *Staying Organized* by Melissa Kelly (n.d.), also included in the References and Additional Resources.

E-PUBLISHING—AN OVERVIEW

The term e-publishing incorporates use of a wide variety of online tools and apps ranging from blogs to e-books. E-publishing—more than other forms of content creation included in this book—relies heavily on use of both computers (desktops or laptops) and tablets. It's possible to do everything on a tablet, but not as efficient or easy as using different kinds of hardware, depending on the complexity of the task at hand. For example, it's easy to blog using a computer or tablet, but writing and publishing an e-book usually works best using a combination of devices.

Blogging isn't a new idea, and teachers might even wonder where it fits into this discussion. Blogs are a good tool for all kinds of writing, because they are readily accessible as well as easy to set up and manage. They can be completely private or fully public, depending on the purpose of the blog. For example, a personal journal would probably have a limited audience, while a blog about classroom news would be more accessible to the public. Students can use blogs to summarize learning, for personal reflection, and for short informal or formal writing assignments. Multiauthor blogs can be used to introduce collaborative writing in a setting where students can comment on one another's posts but not actually edit what someone else has written.

Another tool that can be used on computers and tablets to support student authors is *Google Drive* (formerly *Google Docs*). Originally requiring an online connection to work at all, it's now possible to work offline—primarily for simple editing of a Google Doc—through the Chrome browser (on a computer or Windows 8 tablet) or using the *Google Drive* app (iOS and Android). The option to work offline needs to be selected prior to being offline, but it makes this tool more useful in situations where an Internet connection might not be immediately available. Setting up and using a word processing document is doable on both computers and tablets, but users often prefer to set up spreadsheets, forms, and presentations on a computer initially and then use a tablet for reviewing and very limited editing. These files can be kept private, shared with specific collaborators, or made totally public. A Google Doc is a good place to compose text for e-book publishing.

Educators often think of tablets as substitutes for e-book readers, and tablets can be used for this purpose. By downloading one or more common e-book reader apps (e.g., *iBooks* for iOS only or *Kindle* for iOS, Android, and Windows 8), students can access and read e-textbooks, e-books, pdf files, and other electronic publications. They can also publish and read student-created e-books using computers and tablets. The basic requirement is a tool or app that allows students to write online or convert an existing text file into a readable e-book format, and apps that allow students to access and read e-publications on a tablet.

There are several web-based tools for writing and uploading text that can be formatted and published into one or more e-book formats. Common file formats for e-books include .epub, .pdf, .mobi (or .prc), and .azw (*Kindle*). Depending on the authoring tool used, e-books can include different elements (e.g., illustrations or a table of contents) and be interactive to a larger or smaller degree. Pages can appear to flip, or simply to move from one page to the next with a swipe of the finger. The next section of this chapter includes a brief discussion of the tools needed to create an e-book.

TOOLS AND APPS FOR WRITING AND PUBLISHING

The tools and apps for writing and publishing include a blend of things that work on computers and things that work on tablets. Using the examples provided in the previous section, a computer may be the best option for setting up a blog, an online document, or an e-book, and a tablet can then be used to post updates, make edits, or read the e-book. Alternatively, for users of tablets running iOS, there are a number of apps that allow creation of e-books right on the tablet. On the other hand, while Android and Windows 8 tablets work well for most strategies discussed in this chapter, there is a dearth of apps designed to allow users to create e-books right on these tablets. Here are some of the online tools and apps available for writing and publishing.

Tools and Apps for Blogging

There are blogging sites specifically for student use; the following sites are suggested because they offer apps for two of the three platforms covered in this book.

- *Blogger:* Use the free desktop tool to set up a blog, and then blog on the go using the app for either iOS or Android. There's currently no Windows 8 app, but students can blog within Internet Explorer.
- *WordPress:* Use the free desktop tool to set up a blog. (Check to see if your district or school hosts wordpress.org blogs on a local server; if it does not, ask about using wordpress.com). The free *WordPress* app for Android or iOS supports mobile blogging. There's currently no Windows 8 app, but students can blog within Internet Explorer.

Tools and Apps for Writing and File Management

- *Google Drive:* A free suite of office applications on a computer or tablet. (There's an app for Android and iOS. Access on Windows 8 tablet using Internet Explorer.) If you are using the Chrome browser on a computer or the *Google Drive* app on a tablet, it is possible to do some simple document editing while offline. It also supports collaboration, so multiple authors can work on a file at the same time.
- *CloudOn:* A free office suite app (Android and iOS) that supports creating and editing documents, spreadsheets,

and presentations in MS Office format. Access files through resources like *Dropbox, Box,* and *Google Drive.* Collaboration is not supported at this time, but the Pro version offers additional editing capabilities. Windows RT tablets come with Office preinstalled, and tablets running full Windows 8 can download and run Open Office or equivalent free software suites.

■ *Dropbox* (Android, iOS, and Windows 8): A file hosting service offering cloud storage. A free account includes 2 GB of storage. A *Dropbox* account can be accessed from any Internet-connected device and is useful for accessing and saving files when using a tablet.

■ *Box* (Android, iOS, and Windows 8): Another file hosting service very similar to *Dropbox.* A free account offers a minimum of 5 GB of storage (and up to 50 GB).

Tools and Apps for Publishing E-Books

Most of the following tools are meant to be used on a computer. The resulting publications can usually be downloaded as epub files and then saved to a cloud storage account to be transferred to a tablet for reading.

■ *ePub Bud:* This is a free web-based tool for creating children's picture and chapter books. The e-books created on this site are downloadable in epub format.

■ *My Ebook Maker:* This is another free web-based tool for writing and publishing e-books. It has more sophisticated formatting tools than *ePub Bud* has, but it is still easy to use. These e-books are also downloadable in epub format.

■ *Storybird:* Unlike *ePub Bud* and *My Ebook Maker,* where the author must provide all e-book elements, *Storybird* provides artwork and templates, and authors choose the illustrations they like and write an accompanying story. If you set up a free account, you can save your stories online. Stories can be stored, shared, and read online. However, there is a fee for downloading or printing these e-books. The website works on tablets.

- *Google Story Builder:* This is a very basic free Google app that works on computers and tablets using a web browser. Students identify the characters in a story they would like to write, and then the entire story is told through dialogue. Once completed, it is saved online and viewed as a movie. The author must save the story URL for ongoing access.
- *iBooks Author:* This free Mac app allows users to create interactive multitouch e-books for the iPad. The app works on a Macintosh computer running System OS X 10.7.4 or later. Once published, books can be downloaded from the iBooks Store to be shared and read within this iPad app.
- *Creative Book Builder:* This iOS app costs $3.99. Students can write, edit, and publish e-books in epub format. Published e-books can be read using any reader app that is compatible with epub.
- *Story Kit:* Developed at the University of Maryland's Human–Computer Interaction Lab, this free iOS app is much more simplistic than *Creative Book Builder*, but it can be used to write and illustrate simple e-books. Sound clips can also be added. When finished, the e-book can be uploaded to the *Story Kit* server. A private URL for the story is provided that can be shared with others.

APPS FOR READING E-BOOKS

- *Bluefire Reader:* This free reader (Android and iOS) can be used to read epub, pdf, and Adobe DRM files.
- *iBooks:* This free app for iOS can be used to read e-books available for purchase from the iBooks Store. In addition, epub and pdf files stored in *Dropbox* and similar file hosts can be opened and saved in *iBooks.*
- *Kindle:* Versions of this free app are available for Android, iOS, and Windows 8. It allows for easy access to and reading of pdf files stored in *Dropbox* or *Box.*

There are many other apps for reading e-books. A quick search of the iTunes App Store, Google Play, or the Windows 8 Store will result in a list of apps to choose from. Personal preference and compatible formats are the primary determining factors.

STRATEGIES FOR CLASSROOM USE

When they write, students improve their skills in communication and expression. Writing activities include, but are not limited to, informal journaling, practice in the application of writing mechanics, and formal assignments written individually or collaboratively. Students can engage in writing activities at all grade levels, across all content areas, using various forms of writing. The intended audience for different kinds writing activities will help determine which writing tool is best suited for each occasion. And, depending upon what's available to students, technology can be used in many ways to support these efforts.

Writing assignments designed to ask students to remember or reflect on something individually pretty much require one-to-one access if a tablet or laptop is to be used. When this is possible, a free notes app like *Evernote* or the word processor in an office suite is readily available and offers an easy way for students to write and share files with their teacher. But one-to-one access isn't necessary or even desirable for all types of writing assignments.

When one-to-one access isn't an option, writing assignments can be designed to allow students to rotate through small workstations for individual writing, or to complete activities in small groups, where two to four students collaborate on a writing assignment. In addition, it's not uncommon for students to have more technology access at home than at school via personal devices or technology available through friends, family, public libraries, or other avenues. Survey students to find out what technologies are readily available to them away from school, and use this knowledge while structuring activities.

Of course there needs to be balance between individual and group writing assignments. Each student needs to engage in some kind of writing every day. But don't hesitate to ask them to work together on large projects, such as writing, formatting, publishing, and distributing an e-book.

ACTIVITY SUGGESTIONS

Writing activities go hand in glove with implementation of the Common Core State Standards. Assignments can be tailored to meet performance indicators in any content area. Prior to using tools and apps for independent writing assignments, teachers and students need to become comfortable with their basic operation. And since writing can be supported by a variety of technologies, it may be prudent to tackle one set of tools and apps at a time instead of all of them at once. Even very young children can participate in group writing activities or individual assignments based on emergent writing skills (Benson, 2004). Here are some ideas that can be used by teachers and students.

Build a Google Story: *Google Story Builder* works on computers and tablets. No account or sign-in is required to get started, and it takes just a few minutes to write a story. The final product is a short video clip of the story that appears to be a word processing document being edited. Students compose original stories by selecting characters (up to 10), writing the story in the form of dialogue (up to 10 interactions), choosing a music soundtrack from a list provided by Google, and sharing the story, being sure to copy the URL for later access. There are several ways this tool can be used to support writing. For example, it provides students with practice in writing dialogue, summarizing a reading, and providing an overview of a topic. In addition, teachers can use it to set up a topic for a class discussion.

Character blog: Blogs are often used as personal journals or to post class information, such as homework assignments. Try expanding the use of a blog by setting up several multiauthor blogs based on a piece of fiction or nonfiction being read in class—you want every student to be an author in one of the blogs. Assign each student a character or real person found in the material being read. As reading progresses, post writing prompts based on the reading material, but ask students to reply to the post and other comments as the character they have been assigned. If there are just a few characters, more than one student can be assigned the same one, as long as they are responding in different blogs. This assignment can be taken in a variety of directions depending upon the age and skill levels of students.

Collaborative writing using Google Docs: A Google Doc can be created and edited on a computer or tablet. Depending upon the assignment and students' technology skills, it may be easiest to do initial writing on a computer and then do follow-up work on a tablet, but this is an individual decision. Have students work in writing teams of two to four. At first, you may want to create the Doc they will use and invite each student in as a collaborator (two to four students per document file). Start with a specific assignment; for example, write a poem using a particular format, or write a letter of inquiry requesting information about a location or event. Ask students to work through the five steps of the writing process (prewriting, drafting, revising, proofreading, and publishing) as they work on the assignment. You can incorporate directions and guiding questions in the Doc you distribute to student writing teams to help them navigate the assignment. Remind students that you will be able to review the document history to see who has contributed to the document and what each student has written. Once the team is satisfied with their writing, they can publish it for public viewing. If your students are younger than 13 and your school has not subscribed to Google Apps for Education, they will need to do all their work in a supervised setting to be in compliance with the Children's Online Privacy Protection Act (COPPA).

Publish an e-book: E-book projects can be the work of the entire class, small writing teams, or individual students. Depending upon the structure of the assignment, the complexity of this project can range from fairly simple to quite difficult. Students can write and publish picture books, chapter books, compilations of essays or poetry—whatever is appropriate in your setting. The steps for putting an e-book together include the following:

- Write and edit the text.
- Choose a publishing platform.
- Identify the text elements that will be included (e.g., illustrations, table of contents) depending in part on the platform selected.
- Gather illustrations and other elements.
- Upload files to the publishing platform.
- Publish and share the e-book.

You may want to begin with a class book, where writing teams and/or individuals contribute short pieces of writing, with or without illustrations, to a class collection. Once students are familiar with the process, they can write, publish, and share team or individual e-books.

Writing assignments are limited only by the teacher's imagination. Technology-supported writing brings new dimensions to these critical activities. To learn more, review the entries in the resources section below. You may also find it helpful to review and talk about the discussion points provided here.

Discussion Points

1. Do your students think of themselves as being writers? Why or why not? What can you do to strengthen their perception of the importance of writing?

2. What kinds of writing assignments do you typically make? How could you adapt them to incorporate use of technology? How do you think students would react to the revised assignments?

3. Have you read an e-book? Why or why not? What are the benefits of students being able to publish their writing and read it on a mobile device?

4. Design an activity in which students write and publish an e-book based on a topic of your choice. Once the books are published, post the epub files to share.

REFERENCES AND ADDITIONAL RESOURCES

Apps and reports/articles mentioned in this chapter are listed here, as are additional resources that offer further information about topics discussed in this chapter.

Apps and Tools

Blogger. (Android) http://goo.gl/aTLjC
Blogger. (iOS) http://goo.gl/6tCr6
Bluefire Reader. http://bluefirereader.com
Box. (Android, iOS, and Windows 8) http://www.box.com/
CloudOn. (Android and iOS) http://site.cloudon.com/
Creative Book Builder. (iOS) http://goo.gl/KNGFZ
Dropbox. (Android, iOS, and Windows 8) http://www.dropbox.com
Evernote. (Android, iOS, and Windows 8) http://evernote.com
Google Drive. (Android) http://goo.gl/CS7Nc
Google Drive. (iOS) http://goo.gl/NU6eO
iBooks. (iOS) http://goo.gl/j7WJa
iBooks Author. (Macintosh) http://www.apple.com/ibooks-author/
Kindle. (Android, iOS, and Windows 8) http://goo.gl/FtPLf
Story Kit. (iOS) http://goo.gl/RfhKa
WordPress. (Android and iOS) http://en.support.wordpress.com/apps/

Websites

Blogger. http://www.blogger.com
Children's Online Privacy Protection Act (COPPA). http://www.coppa.org/
ePub Bud. http://www.epubbud.com/
Flipsnack. http://www.flipsnack.com/
Google Drive. https://drive.google.com/#my-drive
Google Story Builder. http://docsstorybuilder.appspot.com/builder

My Ebook Maker. http://www.myebookmaker.com/
Storybird. http://storybird.com
WordPress.com. http://wordpress.com

Online Reports and Articles

Benson, H. (2004, July). *Emergent writing.* PBS Teachers. Retrieved from http://goo.gl/CPV6W

Drennan, M. (2012, July 17). *Blogging in the classroom: Why your students should write online.* Teacher Network. Retrieved from http://goo.gl/5NGaa

How do I incorporate writing into my course without being overwhelmed? (n.d.) Teaching Excellence & Educational Innovation, Carnegie Mellon University. Retrieved from http://goo.gl/fAFbH

Kelly, M. (n.d.). *Staying organized.* Net Places: New Teacher. Retrieved from http://goo.gl/2hync

Responding to writing: Contexts and strategies. (2004). Retrieved from http://goo.gl/zN7qe

Walker, S. (2012, February 23). *5 reasons why your students should write every day.* The Science of Learning Blog. Retrieved from http://goo.gl/L5x8R

Wallace-Segall, R. (2012, October 4). A passionate, unapologetic plea for creative writing in schools. *The Atlantic.* Retrieved from http://goo.gl/X7WRD

Writing Study Group of the NCTE Executive Committee. (2004, November). *NCTE beliefs about the teaching of writing.* National Council of Teachers of English. Retrieved from http://goo.gl/vmCzF

QR Codes in the Classroom

Grade 6 students are studying ancient Egypt. They create displays for a history museum that will be visited by other classes. In addition to the display, each student produces and posts online a video, audio, or text explanation of the display and generates a QR code link. The QR code is printed and included in the display. Now visitors are able to see the displays and independently learn more about each one by scanning the QR codes.

High school students may not be forthcoming about school events, but parents at one high school stay on top of activities and important news using their smartphones and a QR code refrigerator magnet sent home at the start of the school year. Parents know that the school website is updated daily and all they need to do is scan the QR code for immediate access to the latest news. The entry hall at the school also features posters with QR codes linked to clips of student performances, activities, and academic showcases for parents to scan when they are on campus.

From newspapers and magazines to billboards and exhibits in museums, QR codes are cropping up just about everywhere. In a nutshell, these square images are designed to provide quick links to a variety of digital resources such as websites, images, audio recordings, and more. There is a certain amount of "ooh, shiny" factor with QR codes. Kids and adults like scanning them, because it's fun to see where they lead, but classroom use needs to rely on more than novelty. When the primary focus of an activity becomes clever ways to incorporate a new technology rather than learning, educators are allowing themselves to be sidetracked. It's critical to remember that whenever a new technology like QR codes is used, the driving purpose must remain student learning.

Readers may also be asking themselves, "What's the connection between something that offers quick access to digital materials and creating content?" QR codes can be used to extend educators' reach in and outside of the classroom. In addition, students can use them to facilitate demonstrations or presentations of what they have learned. This chapter explores specific ways teachers and students can generate and use QR codes to support teaching and learning. It begins with an explanation of what QR codes are, how to create them, and how they are scanned. The discussion then focuses on strategies for enhancing instruction in the classroom and beyond, along with specific activity suggestions.

QR CODES DEFINED

QR (quick response) codes are two-dimensional, scannable data matrices, the contents of which can be rapidly deciphered using a mobile device that has a camera and an app for scanning the codes. The data in QR codes are arranged using square dots on a square grid. The most common color scheme for QR codes consists of black square dots on a white background. A QR code can store more than 7,000 numeric characters or about 4,300 alphanumeric characters, far more information than can be stored in a UPC barcode (Marquis, 2012).

Originally developed to help track parts in auto manufacturing, QR codes were rapidly adopted for marketing purposes (Burr, 2011). Since then, use of QR codes has pervaded many segments of society. For example, a clothing store asks customers to share outfits they like on social networking sites by scanning a QR code. A car manufacturer encourages potential customers to preview new car features by scanning a QR code that lets them download an app that can be used with the print ad to simulate the effect of these innovations on their driving experience. Additional innovative uses of QR codes in the real world can be found at the web page *Innovative QR Code Campaigns* on the Esponce website.

A QR code is not the same as a bar code. Bar codes are composed of lines. Data are represented by varying the space between the lines and the width of the lines. Bar codes are considered to be one-dimensional and are read using an optical machine—fixed or handheld. Universal product codes (UPCs) are familiar examples of bar codes in the United States. These bar codes include lines and 12 numbers. They are used to track store inventories and for customer checkout.

GENERATING QR CODES

QR codes may appear to be intricate in design, but they are actually quite easy to generate. All you need is the information you want to embed in the QR code and access to a website called a QR code generator. There are many to choose from, and each is either completely free to use or offers free features. While there may be times when it is handy to use a paid feature, educators often find they are able to meet all their QR code generation needs using free sites or the free features on paid sites.

What can be linked to a QR code? An amazing array of digital resources, including website URLs, text messages, voice messages, documents, images, video, virtual business cards, and more. Most, but not all, QR codes require an Internet connection to work. For example, text messages and contact information may be accessible with or without the Internet. More complex digital material may be a paid feature on some QR code generator sites, but a little creative thinking often results in free workarounds. For example, some QR code generator sites charge to link to document files. A no-cost way to link to these files is to post them in a public or shared folder in the cloud using *Dropbox* or a similar service, capture the URL for the uploaded document, and then generate a QR code using that web address.

Different QR code generators offer different features. For example, *Kaywa.com* is very simple. Copy a URL, navigate to *Kaywa.com*, paste the URL in the text box, and a QR code is generated. There are six other types of information that can be made into QR codes using this site, but the options are limited. On the other hand, *QRStuff.com* allows users to create QR code links to a wide variety of digital resources, including websites, text messages, *YouTube* videos, and more.

Some QR code generator sites allow users to change the color scheme of the QR codes from black and white to whatever they would like. Be careful when doing this. In order to be scanned, there must be a sharp contrast between the two colors making up a QR code—which is why black and white is typically the color scheme of choice. If the two colors are closely related (e.g., yellow and orange), the QR code may be unscannable.

In addition to understanding the restrictions of color schemes, it's important to recognize the rationale for the white border that all QR codes have. This border sets the QR code apart from surrounding material and helps ensure that the code can be scanned (Roth, 2011). Every QR code has a square in three of the corners. These squares allow the scanner app to read the QR code no matter how it has been oriented. Use the size of these squares to estimate the size of the border. It should be as wide as one-half the width of one of these small squares in the corner of the QR code. Additional suggestions for using QR codes can be found in *Ten Best Practices for Employing QR Codes* by Brenna Roth (2011).

Once generated, the QR code needs to be captured so it can be printed and used. The easiest way is to right-click on the QR code when it is visible on the computer monitor

(Mac users, hold down the ctrl key while clicking the mouse button), and save the image to the computer in a special folder created for this purpose. Be sure to use a name for each QR code file that will make sense later. A new code does not need to be created every time the same URL or message is used. Instead, open the folder of QR codes, find the desired QR code, open it, copy the image, and paste it into a document or upload it to a web page for ready access.

When printing QR codes for posters, cards, instruction sheets, and such, the image must be crisp and clear. Make sure the ink or toner cartridge is not running low. A smeared or faded QR code will not be scannable.

Here are a few QR code generators educators find useful:

- *Kaywa:* With the free version of this QR code generator, users can make QR codes for seven different kinds of information: URLs, text, SMS, phone numbers, contacts, Facebook pages, and coupons.
- *QRStuff:* The free version of this generator makes it a snap for users to generate QR codes for 20 different kinds of information, including links to social networking sites, video, and much more.
- *QRHacker:* This QR code generator has a free feature that allows users to create a code that includes contact information and embeds a photo of the contact person within the code.
- *QR Voice:* This generator creates free, brief, synthesized voice messages.
- *QR Code Treasure Hunt:* Set up a series of questions, create a QR code for each question, and post codes for students to complete a treasure hunt.

SCANNING QR CODES

Having a QR code to scan is not enough. In order for QR codes to be useful, there needs to be a way to decipher them. This is done through a process called scanning. Most often people use a smartphone, tablet, or similar mobile device with a camera and an app for scanning QR codes. There is a long list of free QR code readers to choose from, but some are better than others. The *i-nigma* app is free, runs on iOS and Android, and tends to be very reliable. *Scan—QR Code and Barcode Reader* is a free app that runs on Windows 8.

To scan a QR code, open the app, point the camera at the QR code, and wait for the app to scan the code. As mentioned earlier, QR codes often require an Internet connection to link to the digital resource, but not always. Text messages and contact information may be accessible offline as well.

Use of a mobile device may be most common, but alternative methods for scanning QR codes are being developed. This is of particular interest to educators whose students may have cell phones with cameras but no data plan, or who may be using a laptop instead of a smaller mobile device. In terms of development, these work-arounds are in their infancy, so reliability may be dicey. However, they are worth a look for students who have no other alternative. For example, *QuickMark* is a free download that allows users to scan QR codes via an image file, a screen capture, or a webcam. There are also extensions for the Chrome browser that make it possible to read QR codes embedded on web pages.

STRATEGIES FOR CLASSROOM USE

Instructional use of QR codes is different from other content creation strategies discussed in this book. In classrooms where teachers and students use QR codes to support creativity and not just automate activities they would have done anyway, careful thought is given to how this goal will be accomplished. To clarify how this can work, think about use of QR codes falling into four categories—extending help to students, sharing important school-related information, enhancing instruction, and formative assessment. Each category incorporates teacher and student use, although some lend themselves more to one target group than the other. Let's take a look at how each can be used in the classroom in general.

Extending help to students: One frustration many teachers express is the inability to respond to individual student questions as quickly as they would like. Often, these questions are about the mechanics of completing work and could be speedily answered if the teacher could just be in two places at once. QR codes facilitate extending teacher reach in the classroom and off campus (assuming the teacher has some kind of web presence or other means of sharing QR codes off campus). Although this use of QR codes may actually address the two lowest levels of the Revised Bloom's Taxonomy (Overbaugh & Schultz, n.d.), by freeing up time that would be eaten up answering basic questions, teachers can devote more of their time to working with students on higher order thinking skills.

What does this look like? Teachers set up learning centers where specific directions can be reviewed by students at any time by scanning one or more QR codes. Activities that require ready access to websites on a variety of Internet-connected devices include QR codes students scan to get to the correct website every time. QR codes linked to a voice synthesizer provide brief audio support to students who need to hear how a word is pronounced, or listen to rather than read directions.

Want to check students' understanding of a concept? Ask them to write directions for how to complete a task and share the directions with the teacher and students using a QR code. By the same token, any of the other general activities mentioned above can be completed by students to demonstrate their understanding of a concept or ability to find resources that support learning.

Encouraging active parent and guardian participation in their children's education is another way teachers extend their reach. Parents who may not have a computer or Internet access at home often have a smartphone with a data plan. Create a QR code to share school contact information, and share it in a classroom newsletter, post it by the classroom door, or make it available through other appropriate venues.

Sharing information: Educators can often do a better job of sharing positive stories about what's happening at school or showcasing student work beyond classroom bulletin boards.

Teachers, administrators, and students themselves use QR codes to facilitate access to information about school and classroom news and student accomplishments. In this case, the QR code is making good news readily accessible to family and community members who are interested in what's happening at school.

Newsletters, student work samples, video or audio recordings, and other information can be posted online, but members of the target audience may not know to check the school or class website. Posters in the school office, hallways, and classrooms that feature QR codes linked to this information are a way to direct traffic to the right place. Or, a QR code for the monthly class newsletter placed on a refrigerator magnet and sent home at the start of the school year offers a ready reminder to scan and check for news regularly. In this case, QR codes offer a pathway to learn about the school community.

Enhancing student learning: In addition to providing answers to basic questions, QR codes are used to enhance instructional materials. For example, a review of a library book might be accessed by scanning a QR code affixed to the back of the book. While reading about metamorphosis, students scan a QR code linked to a video showing the sequence of a caterpillar becoming a butterfly. Or, a student display for a science or social science project includes a QR code linked to a short student-written article about the project. Augmenting materials might initially be done by the teacher, but once students see models of this strategy, they can make contributions themselves.

Formative assessment: Have you seen posters or brochures that pose a yes-or-no question and ask people to scan one QR code if their answer to the question is yes and the other QR code if their answer is no? You can use this same idea in the classroom for formative assessment. A virtual form of the thumbs-up/thumbs-down strategy to check for understanding, QR codes can be used for quick, simple responses to simple questions. They can also be used to allow students to self-check their work, providing immediate feedback and offering a level of autonomy not possible when students have to wait for an adult to tell them the "right" answer to something. Although this strategy does not involve creating something, it does promote independence and can save time by enabling students to check their own work and move on to something else.

ACTIVITY SUGGESTIONS

Of all the content creation strategies outlined in this book, QR code activities are most likely to cross over from instructionally sound activities to technology for the sake of technology. Therefore, planned activities need to be grounded in the four categories of use described in the previous section. In addition, teachers always need to be able to state the instructional objective(s) underlying each activity. Here are some ideas that can be used by teachers and students.

Bulletin board displays: Students often create amazing projects that cannot be physically displayed outside the classroom. Take photos or make a video or audio recording (or some other form of digital documentation of the project), and link it to a QR code. Then have a teacher- or student-created two-dimensional representation of the project that includes the QR code(s). Now students and adults can enjoy the two-dimensional display or scan codes for an enhanced experience. For example, students can design and build a roller coaster and make a video that shows how the roller coaster works. The simple display is their design plan for the roller coaster. The enhanced display is the video of the roller coaster.

New student orientation: Reach out to new students or remind current students about rules and resources on campus by creating a QR code scavenger hunt. Provide a series of questions for which students will need to go somewhere on campus to find the answer. A sample question would be, who do you need to see if you have been absent from school? To find the answer, students would need to go to the office of the attendance clerk and scan a QR code posted there to see if that office represents the correct answer to that question. A QR code scavenger hunt can be expanded to other locations where students spend time, from within a classroom to a venue for a field trip. Once students get the hang of the idea, they can use a QR code generator like *QR Treasure Hunt* to create and deploy their own hunts.

Book reviews: This activity can be done in the library media center or using a classroom library. Ask students to write or record a review for every book they read. Link each review to a QR code, print the code, and affix it to the back of the book. As students browse for new books to read or use for research, they can scan the review codes on the back of the book to see what their peers have to say about it.

Vocabulary activities: Whether it's a word wall display, labeled objects in the classroom, or some other vocabulary exercise, teachers and students can use QR codes to support vocabulary development. For example, label common objects for English language learners, and use a QR code to link each label to an audio message that pronounces the name of the object or uses the name of the object in a short sentence. Post content-specific vocabulary words on a word wall, and ask students to define each word and then check their work by scanning a QR code for each word that shows the correct definition.

Used thoughtfully, QR codes can help teachers support student learning and challenge students to extend their thinking. To learn more, review the entries in the resources section below. You may also find it helpful to review and talk about the discussion points provided here.

Discussion Points

1. Have you ever seen a QR code? Where? What do you think is the underlying purpose for the code(s)?

2. Have you scanned QR codes you've come across? If so, what led you to scan the code(s), and where did the code(s) lead you? If you haven't scanned a QR code, why haven't you?

3. How could you use QR codes at your school to enhance student learning? How would this activity be more than simply automating something you would ask students to do anyway?

4. Design a QR code treasure hunt activity for students based on a topic of your choice. Try it out, and make revisions based on student feedback.

REFERENCES AND ADDITIONAL RESOURCES

Apps and reports/articles mentioned in this chapter are listed here, as are additional resources that offer further information about topics discussed in this chapter.

Apps and Tools

i-nigma. http://www.i-nigma.com/i-nigmahp.html
Scan—QR Code and Barcode Reader. http://goo.gl/IFNtF3

Websites

Innovative QR Code Campaigns. http://www.esponce.com/about-qr-codes
Kaywa. http://qrcode.kaywa.com/
QR Code Treasure Hunt. http://www.classtools.net/QR/
QR Voice. http://qrvoice.net/
QRHacker. http://www.qrhacker.com/
QRStuff. http://www.qrstuff.com/
QuickMark. http://www.quickmark.cn/En/basic/download PC.asp

Online Reports and Articles

Burr, P. L. (2011, November). QR Codes: Effective Web 2.0 classroom tools. *Tech Edge,* pp. 20–21. Retrieved from http://bit.ly/ZtqDM9

Curran, B. (2011, November 16). *Scanning QR codes: No smartphone? No problem!* Engaging Educators. Retrieved from http://bit.ly/XC936G

Marquis, J. (2012, August 27). *Making use of QR codes in education.* Online Universities.com. Retrieved from http://bit.ly/ZtqJmW

McCrea, B. (2011, August 11). QR codes in the classroom. *THE Journal.* Retrieved from http://bit.ly/Ztr3lK

Overbaugh, R., & Schultz, L. (n.d.). *Bloom's Taxonomy.* Old Dominion University. Retrieved from http://ww2.odu.edu/educ/roverbau/Bloom/blooms_taxonomy.htm

QR codes. (2013, February). In *Wikipedia.* Retrieved from http://en.wikipedia.org/wiki/QR_code

Roth, B. (2011, February). *Ten best practices for employing QR codes.* x.commerce. Retrieved from http://go.developer.ebay.com/devzone/articles/10-best-practices-employing-qr-codes

More Ideas for Creating Content

Chapters 2 through 6 discuss ideas for creating content by leveraging common features of tablets using readily available cross-platform apps, using ideas that can be easily implemented across content areas with students of all ages. These suggestions are just the beginning. There are additional ways students can use tablets to create content. Some—such as drawing and painting, animation, music composition, or photo editing—require more background knowledge than is needed to implement the ideas presented in earlier chapters. Others—screencasting, for instance—are platform specific, or at least work better on one platform than others.

As the technology is refined and more apps are developed, additional possibilities for creating content will be uncovered. It's difficult to predict at this time what these improvements might be, but so far app developers have been adept at taking advantage of new capabilities, both in hardware and operating systems. In the meantime, here is a brief overview of a few additional strategies for creating content using existing tablets.

DRAWING

Artists began experimenting with digital art when desktop computers became readily available—the first graphics tablet for home computers, the KoalaPad, was developed in the early 1980s. Graphics tablets interface with a computer. In addition to the tablet, which provides a drawing surface, artists use an implement for drawing or painting. This may be a stylus, a pen, or something called a puck. Graphic tablets also feature a capability called pressure sensitivity which controls line width, transparency, and color.

Shortly after tablets hit the market, artists started exploring ways to use these devices to create art. Portability is a real plus with tablets, and some artists say they prefer smaller devices with screens of seven inches or so. Initially there were more drawing apps for iOS devices than other tablets, but there are a growing number of Android and Windows 8 apps for artists. The main drawback seems to be the lack of pressure sensitivity with tablets, although stylus manufacturers are working on this problem.

Classroom Use

Art teachers who want to offer greater capabilities to serious art students may prefer to explore more sophisticated digital drawing tools like Wacom graphics tablets; one of the pressure sensitive styli now available for iOS, Android, and Windows 8 tablets; and more complex drawing and painting apps. In most other situations, students can use tablets to draw and paint and achieve more than satisfactory results in the process using their fingers or a regular stylus to create art using inexpensive or free apps.

There are many apps currently available in the iTunes App Store or in Google Play. Here are a few recommended for student use:

- *Sketchbook Express:* This free app runs on iOS, Android, and Windows 8 devices and is a great introductory app for students in upper elementary grades and older. A variety of drawing and painting tools and the ability to layer make the app very attractive. A paid version of the app, *Sketchbook Pro* ($4.99), is also available for iOS and Android.

- *Kids Doodle:* A free, cross-platform app (iOS, Android, Windows 8 phone) that allows youngsters to draw on a blank background or photo using brightly colored brushes like neon and rainbow (found in the sliding tray at the bottom of the tablet screen). This app includes a video feature that allows users to finish a drawing and then watch a movie that's a playback of the image being drawn. An ad-free version of the app is available for $0.99.

- *Doodle Buddy:* This free iOS app supports drawing with multiple fingers using various tools like chalk and paintbrush. There is a stamping option, and drawings can be on a plain background or a photo. An ad-free version of the app is available for $0.99.

- *Picasso:* This is a basic free drawing app for Android. Choose from several brush types, select from a plain background or imported photo from the gallery, and start drawing. There are several options for sharing finished artwork.

- *Fresh Paint:* This free basic draw and paint app for Windows 8 is very similar to *MS Paint.* Make custom colors, change brush shape and size, or use various tools like crayons or colored pencils.

Activity Suggestions

Many of the tablet art lesson ideas posted online are based on use of drawing and painting activities that children have done in classrooms for years. Illustrating an alphabet book, designing a poster for a holiday, or drawing a picture in response to a prompt instead of using text are not new ideas necessarily, but use of a drawing app can make it easier to allow students to easily create a piece of art with no muss or fuss.

Drawing and painting apps typically allow young artists to save their drawings directly to the tablet's photo gallery. If that's not the case, snapping a quick screenshot serves the same purpose. Once drawings are finished and saved, it's possible to export them to a computer to use as illustrations for an e-book or to post them on a virtual bulletin board for parents to view.

Artwork saved on a tablet can be imported from the gallery into other apps. For example, students can draw or paint a picture that can be used to explain a concept and then bring that image into a screencasting app (see screencasting discussion below). At that point, the drawing can become the background and be annotated as a narrator explains the concept. In addition, some apps include a mirroring feature. As the artist draws, both the image and its mirror image appear. This feature can be used to teach children about symmetry.

SCREENCASTING

At this time, screencasting is supported on iPads using free or low-cost apps, and there is one paid app, *Explain Everything*, that now offers an Android version. Tablets running the full version of Windows 8 can record screencasts using free tools like *Jing* or *Screenr*, but in this case the screencast is a recording of whatever is on the tablet screen, not the whiteboard environment found in apps for other operating systems. As a result of current limited availability for Android and Windows 8 tablets, this section is devoted to a discussion of screencasting on iPads.

Readers may be familiar with the concept of screencasting on computers using a software program like *Camtasia*

Studio (or *Camtasia for Mac*) or a web-based tool like *Screenr.* When creating a screencast from a computer, the user is making a recording of what appears on the monitor screen in real time. In addition, narration and other sound can be recorded at the same time. Many of the narrated software tutorial videos that are uploaded to sites such as *YouTube* or *Vimeo* were recorded this way. Again, this type of screencasting can be done on a tablet running the full version of Windows 8.

There are two ways to screencast using an iPad. The first uses the built-in AirPlay feature and the mirroring capability of the iPad (generation 2 and later) along with a Wi-Fi connection and a paid software program to make images that appear on the iPad screen also show up on a computer screen. From there, a recording can be made using *Camtasia Studio, Screenr,* or something similar. Two programs that can be used to mirror the iPad's screen image on a computer are:

- *AirServer:* Download this desktop application on three to five computers, depending upon the license purchased. Open the program. With the iPad and computer connected to the same Wi-Fi network, enable *AirPlay* on the iOS device. (See *Using AirPlay* (2013) in the References and Additional Resources section at the end of this chapter.) Tap the name of the computer, and the iPad screen will be mirrored on the computer screen. There are versions for both Mac and PC. The price is $11.99 for the student version and $14.99 for the standard version; group discounts are available for 20 or more licenses.
- *Reflector:* Download this desktop application on one to five computers, depending upon the license purchased. This program operates with the iOS device in the same way as *AirServer.* Versions are available for Mac and PC. The price is $12.99 for an individual computer and $54.99 for a five-seat license.

To record images and narration from the computer screen, use a software program or web-based tool like one of the following:

- *Camtasia Studio* or *Camtasia for Mac:* This software is a screen recorder that allows users to capture video and audio and then edit and produce files that can be shared locally or uploaded to a video hosting site. Education pricing is available.
- *Screenr:* Because it's web-based, this tool works on both Mac and PC. The free version allows users to record screencasts up to five minutes in length. Completed screencasts are hosted on the Screenr site. A paid version is available starting at $19/month.

Using this type of screencast is an excellent way to develop tutorials for how to use an app or how to do something on an iPad, such as work with settings or shut down apps running in the background. Teachers can record videos for students to use or can ask students to demonstrate their mastery of a skill by making a screencast.

The second type of screencast requires use of a free or low-cost app installed on the iPad. A Wi-Fi connection may—or may not—be required, depending on the app. In this case, the app provides a whiteboard-like background on which the user can add text or drawing using fingers, a stylus, or in some cases a text box and the virtual keyboard. Voice can also be recorded. In addition, it is possible to access the camera within the app to take a photo and use it in place of the white background, or to use an image that has been saved in the photo gallery. Some apps even allow users to search online for images to import as a background. These photos can then be annotated during the recording.

Editing within these apps is not supported, but most allow the user to pause the recording, change the background, and then continue recording. When finished, there is a process for uploading the recording to a web-based video host that generates a unique URL for later access.

While there are many commonalities across screencasting apps, there are enough differences that it's worth reviewing several before making a decision about what to use with students. Here are three free apps I regularly use for screencasting on the iPad:

- *ScreenChomp:* Created by TechSmith, the publisher of the *Camtasia* software, this free app does not require a Wi-Fi connection to record, nor do you need to sign up for an account. When there is a Wi-Fi connection, upload completed video files. It is possible to download finish screencasts as mp4 files. With no way to identify the creator of a video, it's important to copy the unique URL right away in order to access it later. Another free screencasting app from these folks is *Ask3.*
- *Educreations:* Users don't need a Wi-Fi connection to record using this app. When a connection is established, new videos will be recorded to the user's free Educreations account. This facilitates access down the road, because videos cannot be downloaded. The website allows users to view screencasts made by other account holders.
- *ShowMe:* Thanks to a fairly recent update, this app does not require a Wi-Fi connection to record video either. Like *Educreations,* users are required to set up a free account, which is used to store all videos made using that account information. *ShowMe* also offers a library of videos created by others that can be viewed and shared.

A paid app popular among many educators is *Explain Everything.* Affordably priced at $2.99 (with a 50% discount for educational institutions), this app offers additional features not found in the free apps. For example, users can import and annotate existing files, including pdf documents and PowerPoint slides.

Screencasting Basics

Screencasting on the iPad is a powerful tool for teachers and students. It enables teachers to extend their reach by making recordings for students and parents to access outside the school day in order to get information or review concepts. Even more important, this capability allows students to work individually or in small groups to demonstrate their understanding by recording themselves talking about topics or explaining ideas for others to view and learn from. Screencasts can be made by students of all ages and can cross all content areas.

The most effective screencasts are brief—five minutes or less. If they are recorded in a classroom, it's a good idea to use earbuds with a built-in microphone to cut down on background noise. A stylus can be easier to use than a finger for writing, but it's probably a time to let personal preference reign. Informal screencasts can be made on the fly, but more formal screencasts require planning, and the quality is usually higher when they are scripted. This is an excellent way to encourage students to work through the writing process, as they don't seem to mind drafting, editing, and proofing text when it's the basis of a screencast script. If they are using an app that requires an account, make sure it is associated with the proper account before recording. If there is no account for the app being used, be sure students know how to find, copy, and paste the URL for later reference.

Activity Suggestions

The ways that teachers and students can use screencasting to create content are nearly limitless. Here are a few ideas to get you started.

Thinking out loud: This diagnostic technique has been around a long time, but it's always been difficult to get around to all students to listen while they talked their way through a task. With screencasting, students can record themselves working through whatever task they've been assigned. Once the screencast is recorded and posted, the teacher can listen and watch when convenient. This technique works anytime the teacher needs to "get inside" a student's head to better understand the student's thought process. Teachers can also model thinking out loud by creating their own screencasts using the technique.

Teach to learn: One of the best ways to master a concept is to figure out a plan for teaching it to someone else. Students can work in small groups to plan and record a screencast that teaches a concept being covered in class. As a bonus, well-done videos can be linked to a class web page for future use.

Project presentation: As an alternative to a class presentation, have students work in small groups to prepare and capture a screencast talk about a project they have completed together. This activity can be used to encourage students to take advantage of the camera to incorporate photos of the process of creating the project. Have videos available for viewing during Open House.

ANIMATING

Even a simple animation can be a labor-intensive endeavor. I'm mentioning it here because animation is a skill that teachers of students in upper elementary grades and higher sometimes opt to use with students. Animation apps do facilitate completion of this type of project, but it is still an activity that will take time to do well.

Classroom Use

Animation offers the opportunity for students to use technology to tell a story about virtually any topic. The animation itself can consist of student-made drawings, predesigned characters and settings, photos of staged scenes—it depends on the purpose of the animation and the app being used. With the exception of *StickDraw,* the apps described here are iOS specific. Those listed below all offer a free version to get users started, but in reality each of them requires users to either upgrade to a full paid version or make in-app purchases to obtain the full suite of desirable basic tools for that particular app. So, try out the free version to see if an app is at all interesting, and then make purchases if warranted.

- *Animation Express:* It's easy to make simple drawings using this iOS app, but it takes a little time to figure out how to take a drawing and turn it into an animation. Documentation is minimal, but once mastered, the app is easy to use.
- *iStopMotion:* A paid app ($9.99), *iStopMotion* offers features beyond those found in free apps. Great for students with more experience in animation.
- *StickDraw:* A free Android equivalent of *Animation Express.*
- *StoMo:* Use this iOS app to make stop motion animations using the tablet cameras (front- or rear-facing). The app is easy to use, in part because special effects are additional purchases.
- Toon Boom apps: This company offers another animation app option, and lite versions of Toon Boom's animation apps are available for iOS and Windows 8. Paid versions ($2.99 each) are available for Android, iOS, and Windows 8.
- *Toontastic:* This iOS app includes predesigned characters and backgrounds, but it also allows users to create their own. Of the four apps mentioned here, this one is the easiest to figure out and use.

Activity Suggestions

Animation provides another venue for students to use when explaining something or telling a story. Project ideas include flipbooks, commercials, public service announcements, and depiction of a process—like the water cycle or metamorphosis. It's a great way to encourage students to walk through the process of planning and executing a video, because it's nearly impossible to wing it when putting together an animated clip.

At a minimum, there needs to be a plot, a storyboard for images, and a script. These requirements alone encourage students to dig more deeply into an activity than they might otherwise. For example, in order to produce a smooth animation, students need to think carefully about the sequence of events they will draw, because if they are not careful, their mistakes will be immediately evident. Addressing this need for attention to detail can be a valuable learning experience for students of all ages.

We are just beginning to realize the possibilities for content creation using tablets. To learn more about the ideas suggested in this chapter, review the entries in the References and Additional Resources section below. You may also find it helpful to review and talk about the discussion points provided here.

Discussion Points

1. Have you used a draw or paint app on a tablet? If not, please try one now. What are the pros and cons of using an app like this to create art?

2. Have you used an app to make a screencast? If not, and if you have access to an iPad, please try one now. How would your students react to using an app like this to create short videos?

3. Have you used an app to make a short animation? If not, please try one now. Is this a practical tool for your students to use? Why or why not?

4. Select one of these tools, and design an activity for your students during which they will use the app to create something. Make a sample of the student product. Try out the activity with your students, and make revisions based on student feedback.

References and Additional Resources

Apps and reports/articles mentioned in this chapter are listed here, as are additional resources that offer further information about topics discussed in this chapter.

Apps and Tools

AirServer. http://www.airserver.com/en/Download
Animation Express. http://goo.gl/eb6mf
Ask3. http://www.techsmith.com/ask3.html
Camtasia Studio. http://www.techsmith.com/camtasia
.html
Educreations. http://www.educreations.com/
Explain Everything. http://www.explaineverything.com/
Fresh Paint. http://goo.gl/01bvS
iStopMotion. http://goo.gl/awfrA
Kids Doodle for Android. http://goo.gl/q9E33
Kids Doodle for iPad. http://goo.gl/hYibe
Kids Doodle for Windows 8 Phone. http://goo.gl/be93M
Reflector. http://www.reflectorapp.com/
ScreenChomp. http://www.techsmith.com/labs.html
ShowMe. http://www.showme.com/
Sketchbook Express for Android. http://goo.gl/lxlxz
Sketchbook Express for iPad. http://goo.gl/R9vBg
Sketchbook Express for Windows 8. http://goo.gl/2DQVf
StickDraw. http://goo.gl/gL6sB
StoMo. http://goo.gl/3GU1Za
Toontastic. http://goo.gl/AzUUn

Websites

Jing. http://www.techsmith.comjing.html
Screenr. http://www.screenr.com/
Toon Boom. https://www.toonboom.com/play/apps

Online Reports and Articles

Agarwal, A. (2012, May 2). *How to record screencast videos on your iPad or iPhone.* Digital Inspiration. Retrieved from http://goo.gl/hbvOl

Animate it! Animation apps for your tablet. (n.d.). Apartment Therapy. Retrieved from http://goo.ghttp://goo.gl/hbvOll/9AA8D

Beeby, V. (n.d.). *How do you doodle on a desktop computer?* Retrieved from http://goo.gl/Hhm0d

Chinavasion33. (2013, January 3). *Art attack—Five free Android tablet apps for the budding artist.* GoArticles.com. Retrieved from http://goo.gl/f5EuB

Creating iPad screencasts. (n.d.). Mac Sage. Retrieved from http://goo.gl/57Jjx

Henry, A. (2012, May 27). *Five best tablet drawing apps.* Lifehacker. Retrieved from http://goo.gl/CPLEV

Isaac, M. (2011, July 19). *Exclusive: Drawing app for artists debuts on Android tablets.*Wired.com. Retrieved from http://goo.gl/QZFXV

Shaik, A. I. (2013, February 28). *Rise of content creation in tablets and smartphones.* TechNews Report. Retrieved from http:// http://goo.gl/hbvOlgoo.gl/jrM9j

Silbert, S. (2011, May 6). *Help me LAPTOP: I need a tablet for creating digital art.* LAPTOP. Retrieved from http://goo.gl/bgBb5

Tablet apps for art making fun. (n.d.). Apartment Therapy. Retrieved from http://goo.gl/FRMEm

Tavakoli-Far, P. L. (2012, October 22). *Creating art on tablets remains a work in progress.* BBC News Technology. Retrieved from http://goo.gl/V9xx0

Thomas, A. (2010, July 24). *Digital artists create iPad masterpieces.* Techradar.Computing. Retrieved from http://goo.gl/Izhpn

Ulanoff, L. (2010, October 5). *Learning to draw on the iPad.* PCMag.com. Retrieved from http://goo.gl/b890

Using AirPlay. (2013). Apple Inc. Retrieved from http://support.apple.com/kb/ht4437

Incorporating Tablets Into Instruction

R esearch going back to the mid-1990s shows that when educators learn how to use a new technology, there are several stages of use they work through before they are ready to make best use of the new technology to support student learning. Initial stages of use focus on personal benefit and then automation of traditional instructional activities before educators are ready to use the technology in significantly new or different ways. Other research establishes that the best technology-supported instructional plans balance use of technology with incorporation of academic content and effective instructional strategies.

There is nothing wrong with rudimentary use of technology at the beginning, but it's important to understand that until more advanced levels of use are achieved, incorporation of the technology has little or no impact on student achievement. Links to well-known examples of this research are included in the References and Additional Resources section at the end of this chapter. It's worth taking time to review these findings and models before reading the rest of this chapter. Here's a quick list of suggestions. (Links are in the References and Additional Resources section):

- *LoTi Digital-Age Framework:* This includes the Levels of Technology Implementation Scale (LoTi), originally developed in 1994 by Dr. Christopher Moersch. Aligned with the Apple Classrooms of Tomorrow research, this scale identifies six levels of use of technology in the classroom.
- *Changing the Conversation About Teaching, Learning, and Technology: A Report on 10 Years of ACOT Research:* This is the final report for the Apple Classrooms of Tomorrow project (ACOT); it identifies a progression of five stages of use educators move through as they adopt and use new technologies with students.
- *SAMR Model:* Developed in 2006 and aligned with the ACOT research, this model includes four levels of technology use in classrooms.
- *TPACK Model:* Also developed in 2006, TPACK provides a framework that can be used to determine the level of technology integration taking place in a classroom.

As you review the research, think about how this information relates to designing learning activities to support classroom use of tablets.

What's an *Apptivity?*

Although it sometimes refers to use of toys that work in conjunction with an iPad app, the term *apptivity* was originally coined by a group of educators during a summer institute for Apple Distinguished Educators (ADEs). The ADEs used to meet annually to collaborate on designing and completing projects, and in the wake of the release of the first iPad, the group that met in 2010 decided to focus on ways iPads could be used to change teaching and learning. The result of their efforts was an online collection of more than 50 sample lessons, or apptivities, that can be used to help K–12 educators develop activities of their own that support classroom instruction. The website has not been updated recently, but it is still a valuable resource for educators to use as a springboard for their own apptivity planning. Visit the site to see sample apptivities for primary grades through high school.

Why coin a new term to describe classroom activities that incorporate touch technology? It may not be absolutely necessary, but I think it helps educators differentiate between use of technology to automate traditional activities and use of one or more apps to approach learning in new or enhanced ways. Keeping this alternative perspective in mind and remembering the findings of the research mentioned earlier, the remainder of this chapter focuses on planning instructional activities that makes effective use of mobile apps.

APPTIVITY PLANNING

It's tempting to introduce tablets into classrooms because they're fun and engaging. There's nothing wrong with fun or engagement, but the driving force behind any instructional activity must be the curriculum. Chapter 1 presents rubrics and checklists for choosing high-quality apps that support the curriculum. In this chapter the assumption is made that the teacher has already

- identified the content standard(s) and performance indicator(s) to be addressed,
- reviewed a list of possible apps, and
- used a checklist or rubric to narrow down the list to one to three apps.

Unless the teacher works in one of the states that has not adopted the Common Core State Standards (CCSS), math and language arts apptivities will most likely be based on CCSS. Standards and performance indicators for apptivities grounded in other academic areas will be drawn from state frameworks.

The planning template presented below consists of three sections. The first part focuses on overall apptivity design, the second on instructional specifics, and the third on classroom management. For purposes of the discussion here, the form is literally divided into three parts. The entire form is available at the end of the chapter.

Overall Apptivity Design

This approach to planning relies on familiarity with the TPACK model (Baran, Hsueh-Hua, & Thompson, 2011), the Revised Bloom's Taxonomy (Overbaugh & Schultz, n.d.), and levels of technology use as identified in the research. In the beginning, the level of detail and time required to complete this form may remind educators of their first year of teaching. Effective use of any technology requires a different approach to instruction, and this is challenging to veteran and novice educators alike, because they cannot rely solely on their past experience.

To successfully integrate tablets into classroom learning, use of the technology must be interwoven to the point that it would be difficult or even impossible to teach the lesson in the same way if the technology were not available. This shift from technology as a tool to simply automate an activity to technology as an integral part of the instructional delivery system is discussed in the ACOT research explanation of the differences between the third and fourth stages of use. This does not mean that the elements of apptivity design will be unfamiliar to teachers, but it does mean that these elements need to be considered from a different point of view.

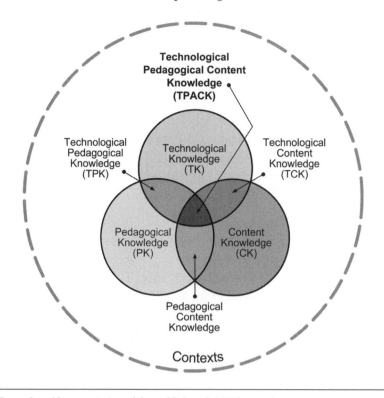

Reproduced by permission of the publisher, © 2012 by tpack.org

The first section of the planning form lays the overall groundwork for the apptivity. The following narrative walks the reader through each field in this section of the form.

1.   Content area standard(s) and supporting performance indicator(s): Based on the premise that use of tablets must be driven by the curriculum, begin by identifying the content area standard and supporting performance indicators that drive the apptivity. This step also addresses one of the three domains of the TPACK model—content.

2.   Pedagogy: What instructional strategies will be used during the apptivity? This item addresses the second domain of the TPACK model—pedagogy.

3.   Technology: What technology will be used to support the lesson? For lessons stemming from information in this book, it's a given that the hardware used will be a tablet or some other type of mobile touch technology. Therefore, technology-related decisions will focus on the apps used on these devices. It is assumed that the apps selected have already been reviewed using a rubric or checklist to ensure quality and a connection to the curriculum. This item addresses the remaining domain of the TPACK model—technology.

4.   Level(s) of the Revised Bloom's Taxonomy: Once the three elements of the TPACK model are identified, the educator is asked to note which level of the Revised Bloom's Taxonomy is targeted in the apptivity. This is an important question. Sometimes educators assume that virtually any use of technology will encourage students to use higher order thinking skills, but nothing could be further from the truth. Many common instructional uses of technology actually address the three lowest levels of the taxonomy. There's nothing inherently wrong with this, as long as the teacher recognizes that this is the case and has made an intentional decision to have students work at these levels for a specific reason. Reflecting on where an apptivity falls in the Revised Bloom's Taxonomy encourages teachers to target more than the first three levels of the taxonomy.

5.   Apptivity objective(s): The overall design section of the planning form ends with asking the educator to develop a measurable objective for the apptivity. *Measurable* is the key term here. In order to develop an assessment plan for the apptivity, there must be a clearly stated objective that can be attained by completing the apptivity within the time allotted. The primary objective should be tied to the content standard/performance indicator(s). There could be a secondary measurable objective related to a technology use skill.

Apptivity title:	
Teacher name:	Grade level(s):
Time required to complete this apptivity:	
Overall Apptivity Design	
Content area standard(s) and supporting performance indicator(s)	Enter each standard and its supporting performance indicator(s) here.
Pedagogy	Describe the instructional strategies you will use during this apptivity to leverage use of the technology.
Technology	Identify the specific technology used during the apptivity (e.g., hardware, software, or app).
Level(s) of the Revised Bloom's Taxonomy	Use this area to identify the level of the Revised Bloom's Taxonomy addressed in this apptivity.
Apptivity Objective(s)	Use this area to list the objective(s) for the apptivity.

Apptivity Specifics

The second section of the planning form is an outline of the apptivity. There are numerous models for basic lesson design—this form includes lesson components typically found in most of these models, although they may be called something different. The components included here will be familiar to experienced teachers. What's different is how each is framed within the apptivity, keeping in mind the stages of use of technology identified in research. Just as it's easy to inadvertently confine apptivities to the lower three levels of the Revised Bloom's Taxonomy, it's also common for apptivities to be based on the earliest stages of technology use. Equally important is the inclusion of a sample product. Not only does this help the teacher ensure that the apptivity works, it also provides a model for students and colleagues. Here is a brief walk-though of each field in this section of the form.

1. Introduction to apptivity: How will students' attention be captured? How will the apptivity be tied to the content and made relevant for students?

2. Apptivity description: This section consists of multiple steps. It includes a clear description of the instructional strategies the teacher plans to use—how the materials are introduced and reviewed, and what students do as they work to meet the apptivity objective(s). It may be helpful to visit the Learning Activity Types Wiki to review ideas related to TPACK. Initially, it may be helpful to create a flowchart instead of a list of steps. A flowchart helps teachers develop contingency plans in case there's a problem with the technology or students react in an unexpected way.

3. Assessment of apptivity: Formative and summative assessment are critical aspects of instruction. This component asks teachers to identify strategies for monitoring student performance during and after the apptivity. The assessments can be formal, informal, or a combination of both.

4. Apptivity extensions: This component identifies ways the apptivity will be adjusted to meet individual student needs. Some will require additional support through scaffolding, while others will need challenges that will hold their interest.

5. Link to sample: As mentioned above, it is important to create a sample of the final student product. This can be created by the teacher or a student volunteer. Not only does this provide a model for students, it also serves as a check to ensure planned apptivity steps will actually work.

Apptivity Specifics	
Introduction to apptivity	Use this area to add the apptivity introduction.
Apptivity description	Use this area to specifically describe the steps for completing the apptivity.
Assessment of apptivity	Use this area to describe how student work will be assessed.
Apptivity extensions	Use this area to add lesson extensions.
Link to teacher or student-created sample:	

Apptivity Implementation

The final section of the planning form focuses on apptivity implementation: how the technology is used by teachers and students, the materials required, and preparations that need to be made ahead of time. This section may seem overmuch to the experienced teacher. However, it has been my experience that use of tablet technology for instruction is unfamiliar enough that it is deceptively easy to over- or underestimate what's required when first incorporating its use. No matter how thorough the planning, mistakes will be made, and there will be unanticipated outcomes. Nevertheless, teachers who take the time to think deeply about the specifics of how the technology will be used, how they will manage the classroom, what materials they will need, and what preparation is required can make great strides toward ensuring that implementation proceeds as smoothly as possible.

1.   How the teacher uses technology: As educators plan for how they will use technology during the class, it is beneficial to refer to the research on teachers and stages of technology use. This includes Apple's Classrooms of Tomorrow report and the SAMR model. The reasoning behind this suggestion is that although a teacher may conclude that use at an earlier stage is appropriate, this needs to be a conscious decision. The plan should include a brief, but specific, description of how the adult(s) in the room will use technology.

2.   **How the students use technology:** The next step then is to describe how students will use the technology. Again, teachers should refer to the research on stages of use and ensure that the apptivity targets the level of use intended.

3.   **Classroom management techniques:** Decisions about how the technology will be used will impact how the technology is managed. The premise throughout this book has been that one-to-one can be the exception, not the norm, in most cases. This field provides an opportunity for teachers to think through and document how groups will be formed, tasks will be assigned, commonalities across platforms will be leveraged, and so on.

4.   **Materials:** This may seem like a no-brainer, but teachers new to apptivities often miss the basics such as students needing to have a particular app or device in order to complete the lesson. Also, apptivities often rely on offline supporting materials. So teachers should take the time to make a list here.

5.   **Preparation before class:** Again, although this may seem painfully obvious, it's easy to forget that an app needs to be downloaded, or offline support materials need to be prepared ahead of time. A list now will avoid problems later.

Apptivity Implementation	
How the teacher uses technology	Use this area to describe how and when the teacher uses technology during the apptivity.
How the students use technology	Use this area to describe how and when students use technology during the apptivity.
Classroom management techniques	Use this area to explain accommodations for technology use, student grouping, etc.
Materials	Use this area to list all required materials.
Preparation before class	Use this area to list all tasks to be done prior to teaching the apptivity.
Additional notes:	

In Summary

Nothing, including the information in this book and the planning form presented here, is a guaranteed prescription for integrating tablet devices into classrooms. In fact, it is entirely possible to use the apps described in earlier chapters and the planning form to develop apptivities that do nothing more than automate tasks that could be done as easily with paper and pencil. Use at this level may initially capture the interest of disengaged students who need to review and practice specific skills, but if this is the only way technology is used in class, students will quickly lose interest.

Planning apptivities that incorporate more sophisticated levels of use and higher order thinking skills takes time and a great deal of thought. Most teachers will probably want to move gradually into this type of use. But those who do take up the challenge will reap great rewards and benefits, not just for their students, but for their own professional practice as well.

Complete Apptivity Planning Form

As promised at the beginning of this chapter, here is the complete planning form in one table. Readers may also access an electronic version of the form using the following URL: http://goo.gl/3M8euG

Apptivity title:	
Teacher name:	Grade level(s):
Time required to complete this apptivity:	
Overall Apptivity Design	
Content area standard(s) and supporting performance indicator(s)	Enter each standard and its supporting performance indicator(s) here.
Pedagogy	Describe the instructional strategies you will use during this apptivity to leverage use of the technology.

Technology	Identify the specific technology used during the apptivity (e.g, hardware, software, or app)
Level(s) of the Revised Bloom's Taxonomy	Use this area to identify the level of the Revised Bloom's Taxonomy addressed in this apptivity.
Apptivity objective(s)	Use this area to list the objective for the apptivity.
Apptivity Specifics	
Introduction to apptivity	Use this area to add the apptivity introduction.
Apptivity description	Use this area to specifically describe the steps for completing the apptivity.
Assessment of apptivity	Use this area to describe how student work will be assessed.
Apptivity extensions	Use this area to add lesson extensions.
Link to teacher or student-created sample:	
Apptivity Implementation	
How the teacher uses technology	Use this area to describe how and when the teacher uses technology during the apptivity.
How the students use technology	Use this area to describe how and when students use technology during the apptivity.
Classroom management techniques	Use this area to explain accommodations for technology use, student grouping, etc.
Materials	Use this area to list all required materials.
Preparation before class	Use this area to list all tasks to be done prior to teaching the apptivity.
Additional notes:	

Discussion Points

1. Review the resources related to the TPACK model. How does this information change your thinking about designing technology-supported instruction?

2. Review the resources related to the Apple Classrooms of Tomorrow report and the SAMR model. Where would you place yourself on either scale relative to your use of tablet devices as a tool for teaching and learning? Explain your answer.

3. Use the planning tool to design an apptivity. Share your completed plan with a colleague and ask for feedback. What revisions will you make based on the response you receive?

4. Now introduce the apptivity you developed to students. Write a reflection about how it went. What worked? What would you change before using the apptivity again? How did your students react to the apptivity?

References and Additional Resources

Websites and reports/articles mentioned in this chapter are listed here, as are additional resources that offer further information about topics discussed in this chapter.

Websites

Apptivities. http://www.apptivities.org/
Bloom's Taxonomy. http://goo.gl/MQjNv
Common Core State Standards Initiative. http://www.corestandards.org/
Learning Activity Types Wiki. http://activitytypes.wmwikis.net/
TPACK. http://tpack.org/

Online Reports and Articles

Baran, E., Hsueh-Hua C., & Thompson, A. (2011, October). TPACK: An emerging research and development tool for teacher educators. *TOJET: The Turkish Online Journal of Educational Technology, 10*(4). Retrieved from http://bit.ly/15qnKPx

Changing the Conversation about Teaching, Learning, and Technology: A Report on 10 Years of ACOT Research. (1995). Apple Computer, Inc. Retrieved from http://bit.ly/YVhQEa

Loader, D. (2012). *Applying the SAMR model into education.* Adobe Systems, Inc. Retrieved from http://adobe.ly/15qoOmr

LoTi Digital-Age Framework. (2011). LoTi, Inc. Retrieved from http://bit.ly/15qp6tH

Overbaugh, R., & Schultz, L. (n.d.). *Bloom's Taxonomy.* Old Dominion University. Retrieved from http://ww2.odu.edu/educ/roverbau/Bloom/blooms_taxonomy.htm

Index

CORWIN
A SAGE Company

The Corwin logo—a raven striding across an open book—represents the union of courage and learning. Corwin is committed to improving education for all learners by publishing books and other professional development resources for those serving the field of PreK–12 education. By providing practical, hands-on materials, Corwin continues to carry out the promise of its motto: **"Helping Educators Do Their Work Better."**